The
Connell Guide
to
Shakespeare's

_____

Hamlet

_____

by
Graham Bradshaw

Contents

NOTES

Introduction

In the four centuries since Shakespeare's death in 1616, *Hamlet* has almost always been regarded as Shakespeare's greatest play. This in itself is not surprising. As Barbara Everett has observed, *Hamlet* was not only "the first great tragedy in Europe for two thousand years"; it was, and still is, "the world's most sheerly entertaining tragedy, the cleverest, perhaps even the funniest".

Once the news got round among Elizabethan theatre-goers of Shakespeare's decision to revise an earlier, now lost, play called *Hamlet* it must have surprised them, just as modern theatre-goers would have been surprised if Samuel Beckett had decided to produce a new version of Agatha Christie's *The Mousetrap*. When Shakespeare's play was first performed, many in the audience would have seen – or at least known – what happened in this older but far from old *Hamlet*, which was in existence by 1589 and still being performed in the early 1590s. Surviving references to the earlier play confirm that it was popular and highly melodramatic. The Ghost in the early version, for example (dismissed by one critic for the way he cries "Revenge! Revenge!" like an "oyster-wife" – at a time when oysters were cheap), was hardly the imposingly mysterious figure Shakespeare created.

Nor was the central figure more than a shadow

of the character Shakespeare was to create. While we now use the phrase "Hamlet without the Prince" to refer to something unimaginable, like an omelette without eggs, the play that Shakespeare had chosen to revise was also a *Hamlet* without the prince – or without *his* Prince, a character who utterly dominates the play he so reluctantly inhabits to a degree that is rivalled only by Prospero in *The Tempest*. Even when Hamlet isn't on stage, speaking nearly 40% of the play's text, the other characters are talking and worrying about him.

This is the most obvious reason why – as the Spanish poet and diplomat Salvador de Madariaga observed at the beginning of his splendidly provocative book *On Hamlet* – the chief trouble in the history of *Hamlet* criticism has been that it is so Hamlet-centred: many critics, from Coleridge through to A. C. Bradley and beyond, see the play and its other characters almost entirely through Hamlet's eyes.

Yet the play is no exception to – and indeed can be seen as an extreme example of – Shakespeare's usual dramatic method, which was never to press or even reveal his own view on controversial issues like the divine right of kings or honour or ghosts and purgatory, but to "frame" these issues by assembling characters who think and feel differently about them. This is what sets a Shakespearean "play of ideas" apart from a "play of ideas" by, say, Ibsen or Bernard Shaw. It is usually easy to see what these later dramatists think about the issues they are dramatising. But with Shakespeare it is very hard, even impossible, to know what he thinks about (say) revenge or incest or suicide – and Hamlet's view is often strikingly different from the views of those around him.

If we take suicide, we find all kinds of different attitudes expressed to it in Shakespeare's work, and Hamlet himself sees it in different ways in his first soliloquy – and in his fourth, the most famous of all soliloquies. In the first ("O that this too too solid flesh would melt...") he takes God's prohibition of revenge to be decisive. In the fourth ("To be or not to be...") he does not even refer to God.

Or take revenge. While a divine prohibition of suicide is nowhere to be found in the Old or New Testaments, God's prohibition of revenge is not in doubt: "Vengeance is mine, saith the Lord; I will repay." Hamlet, however, barely discusses revenge and never takes a coherent view on it. Indeed he is torn between opposing views in a play which includes three sons whose fathers have been killed (Fortinbras, Hamlet and Laertes) – and who think and react very differently. At least they *can* act differently, whereas the daughter who has lost her father can only react by going mad – and (probably) committing suicide.

Sometimes it almost seems as though a Shakespearean play of ideas is doing its own "thinking", with the playwright orchestrating intensely divisive either-or alternatives that academic critics can then debate very intensely, with much flaring of gowns. Is Shylock a black-hearted villain or a crypto-tragic victim? Is Henry V the mirror of a Christian King, or a cold-hearted Machiavellian manipulator? Is Othello a "Noble Moor" or a deluded egotist? And it is these debates which make the plays so exciting. If the doubts about whether the Ghost in *Hamlet* is the messenger of divine justice or a devilish instrument of damnation were ever finally resolved, the play would be diminished, or shrivel into a museum piece. This short guide deliberately targets "traditional" ways of seeing the play and some of its arguments will seem unorthodox and even heretical. But I have taken pains to set such views alongside views that are more familiar and indeed traditional, leaving you in the end – as Shakespeare himself did – to make up your own mind.

A summary of the plot

Although editors divided *Hamlet* into five acts, the play is structured in three movements, each of which covers a startlingly short period of time. In each movement the scenes follow each other very rapidly, with no longer break than the nights in which the characters are sleeping, or trying to. The first critic to see this was the distinguished actor, producer, director and playwright Harley Granville-Barker in his *Preface to Hamlet*(1936). Although the 1605 Second Quarto and the 1623 First Folio texts (the two most authoritative early texts of *Hamlet*) differ in many ways, the three movement structure is apparent in both: the first spans two nights and one day; the second, two months later, spans three days; the third two days.

The first movement

The first movement has five scenes and, as Granville-Barker dryly puts it, "coincides with the first act of the editors". This movement begins at midnight on the castle ramparts where it will also end, a day and a night later.

The sentries are clearly very frightened about something. The actor playing Francisco, the sentry who is being relieved by Barnardo, has a tiny part, but it includes the unforgettable lines:

> *For this relief much thanks. 'Tis bitter cold,*
> *And I am sick at heart.*

It soon becomes clear that a Ghost or "thing" has appeared on the two previous nights. When Marcellus – the most thoughtful and vocal of the sentries – arrives he has brought the learned and sceptical Horatio with him. Marcellus tells Barnardo that he "entreated" Horatio to join them so that he can "approve our eyes" if the "thing" appears again, and because Horatio is a scholar who will know how to address the "thing". Horatio insists that it is their "fantasy" and that it will "not appear again" – whereupon it does, as every theatre-goer would expect. But once again it stalks off without speaking.

In the anxious discussion that follows, the thoughtful Marcellus wonders whether the thing's appearance might be connected with the alarmingly mysterious, pell-mell way in which the country has been preparing for war: "tell me he that knows". The well-informed Horatio then explains "how the whisper goes" in a long story that introduces the play's important political theme.

Thirty years ago old King Hamlet had accepted a challenge to personal combat from King Fortinbras of Norway, who then lost Norwegian "lands" as well as his life. Denmark is now threatened with an invasion since young Fortinbras, who is not King of Norway, has "shark'd up" an army of "landless resolutes" so that he can avenge his father and reclaim the lost lands.

Although these thoughtful men all agree that the "thing" looks "like" King Hamlet they never once suppose that it is what it tells Hamlet it is, "thy father's spirit". They all suspect it is demonic. It is important to notice this, since 19th century critics always assumed – as did important 20th century critics like A.C. Bradley and Stephen Greenblatt – that the "thing" just is the Ghost of Hamlet's father.

At this point the "thing" re-appears, to everybody's amazement, but stalks away again without speaking. Dawn is breaking, and Horatio and Marcellus set off to find young Hamlet and tell him what they have seen.

The second scene begins with what is evidently the new King Claudius's first Council meeting. The main item on the agenda is the threat of invasion from Norway, which the King has already all but contained – through an impressive combination of diplomacy and craft. The new king is not an old-style warrior king, like his dead brother, whose widow Claudius has married.

Hamlet, in a black mourning cloak, is grieving for his dead father, and when he is left alone his torrential first soliloquy explodes with his feelings about his mother's second marriage, a marriage which took place so soon after his father's death. Horatio and Marcellus then arrive to tell him about the Ghost, and he promises to join them on the ramparts.

In the next scene, Ophelia, the daughter of Claudius's Lord Chamberlain, Polonius, is warned by both her father and her brother, Laertes, to be wary of Hamlet's talk of love: Hamlet's royal duties mean she will eventually be cast aside. Her father's onslaught is so fierce that she promises to break off communications with the Prince. (By the end of the play Polonius's family will all be dead, with Hamlet directly or indirectly responsible.)

The fourth scene begins at midnight on the second night, when Hamlet joins Horatio and Marcellus on the ramparts, and the first movement's climax comes in its fifth scene when the "thing" finally speaks. Hamlet has already been shattered before he meets the Ghost. Now he is shattered again as he is given the "dread command" to kill the new king, Claudius. Claudius, he is told, murdered his brother, Hamlet's father, by pouring poison into his ear – and had been sleeping with Hamlet's mother even before the murder. As Hamlet later puts it, Claudius "killed my King and whored my mother".

The second movement

When the second movement begins it is quietly established that time has passed since the first. Laertes is back in Paris and in need of more funds from his father. The ambassadors have just returned from Norway. Rosencrantz and Guildenstern have arrived from Wittenberg, after being "sent for" by Claudius. Just how much time has passed is only established much later in the

Mousetrap scene (3.2): when the "mad" Hamlet says to the astonished Ophelia, "look how cheerfully my mother looks, and my father died within's two hours", she replies: "Nay, 'tis twice two months, my lord." Her elegantly phrased reply helps us to put this together: there is an interval of two months between the death of Hamlet's father and the beginning of the play, and another two months pass between the play's first and second movements. As Granville-Barker brilliantly shows, Shakespeare wants to indicate the passage of time in natural, unobtrusive ways.

The first scene in the second movement is short and in two parts. Polonius is both funny and morally unpleasant – furthering the play's exploration of notions of honour – when he tells Reynaldo he must go to Laertes and spy on him there, using underhand methods if necessary. Polonius also hears from Ophelia of Hamlet's distracted behaviour. This alarms Polonius because he himself had insisted that Ophelia break off private communications with the Prince, which she has done for the last two months – and now the Prince is more mad than ever. Polonius heads off to tell the King that he has discovered the cause of Hamlet's madness.

The King and Queen welcome Rosencrantz and Guildenstern in the next scene, and Claudius tells them he hopes that they can discover the reason for Hamlet's "transformation". When they leave to find Hamlet, Polonius explains his new theory:

Hamlet, he says, is mad with love for Ophelia. The Queen still thinks Hamlet's behaviour is due to his father's death and her "o'erhasty" re-marriage to Claudius, but she doesn't dismiss Polonius's theory, and Claudius and Polonius make a plan for Hamlet to meet Ophelia again so they can eavesdrop on what is said.

In the two months that have passed since the Ghost issued its "dread command", Hamlet has done nothing except feign madness; he himself is, as he says, "lapsed in time". When a company of Players arrives at court Hamlet decides that they can stage a play which will test whether or not the Ghost was telling the truth. During the performance of the play, Claudius responds in a way which convinces Hamlet (though not Horatio) that Claudius did murder his father. Hamlet, however, has made no plan about what he should now do. Shakespeare's plays, and not just his tragedies, typically build towards a climax – in Hamlet, the climax comes in Act Three, scene two, then spreads through the two scenes which follow: the so-called prayer scene, and the so-called closet scene where Hamlet has a searing encounter with his mother. Not surprisingly, many Freudian critics see this as the most important scene of the play.

When he finds the defenceless Claudius on his knees in the prayer scene, he doesn't kill him, or confront him. Instead he goes off to meet his mother in the closet scene, and we hear him calling

"Mother, mother, mother!" from "Within", while he is still offstage.

Soon after this scene begins Hamlet butchers Polonius, who is hiding behind an arras – Hamlet thinks he is stabbing the king – and having done so makes a morbid joke about it.

> *Thou wretched, rash, intruding fool, farewell;*
> *I took thee for thy better; take thy fortune;*
> *Thou find'st to be too busy is some danger.*

The second movement finally ends when Hamlet sees Fortinbras's army entering Denmark as he leaves for England, where Claudius has now planned that Hamlet will be killed.

The third movement

The third movement begins in Act Four, scene five and, as in the first movement, there are five scenes. The tension rebuilds at once. Poor Ophelia has gone mad. Laertes arrives from Paris, infuriated by his father's death and "hugger-mugger" burial, and leading an army of rebellious Danes who cry "Laertes shall be king!"

In the closet scene Hamlet had berated his mother, telling her she must stop sleeping with Claudius. "Refrain tonight," he says, "And that shall lend a kind of easiness / To the next abstinence" – as though he were telling her how to stop smoking. But when it looks as though Laertes will kill Claudius she rushes to defend him by holding on to Laertes. She obviously still loves Claudius, who shows himself perfectly able to deal with Laertes and "calm his rage". He plots with Laertes to have Hamlet killed in a fencing match – Laertes's sword is to have a poisoned tip.

Hamlet, meanwhile, has discovered the plot against his life and arranged for Rosencrantz and Guildenstern to be killed instead. On arrival back at Elsinore, he goes to the graveyard to meet Horatio and encounters the gravediggers. The gravediggers discuss Ophelia's apparent suicide by drowning and produce a skull belonging to the King's former jester, Yorick, and Hamlet addresses it, ruminating about death. Laertes arrives, and he and Hamlet fight in Ophelia's grave. Amazingly, since Claudius and Laertes are both in such a hurry to kill Hamlet, the final duel takes place later on the same day Ophelia is buried.

The catastrophe with which the play ends comes as a wild series of accidents. Gertrude drinks from a poisoned cup meant for Hamlet and dies. Learning that the man she loved had meant to poison her son is her final agony, unless she is still alive to hear her son's brief and pitiless farewell: "Wretched mother adieu." Hamlet wins the first two rounds against Laertes, but then Laertes stabs or cuts Hamlet before the third round.

A furious scuffle follows, from which Hamlet emerges with Laertes's sword – whether by accident or design. Hamlet then knows that Laertes's sword is "unbated", or untipped, but he doesn't know that it is envenomed and that he is now dying. Some stage Hamlets then cut or wound Laertes, while others are so enraged that they run him through. The dying Gertrude tells Hamlet that the drink was "poisoned", and Laertes tells him that the sword is envenomed, that they are now both dying, and that "the king's to blame".

Hamlet immediately stabs Claudius with the same sword, forces the rest of the poisoned drink down his throat, and tells him to "follow my mother". There is little or no sense that he is finally carrying out the Ghost's "dread command", since Hamlet never says (and the Court doesn't know) that he is killing the man who "killed my king". If the deeply religious Hamlet we saw in the play's second scene had known that he had "not half an hour of life", he would have immediately called for a priest. But now his final act, before dying himself, is to give his "dying voice" to young Fortinbras as the next King of Denmark – so that the Tragedy of Hamlet includes the Tragedy of Denmark. The third movement then comes to an end. To quote Hamlet's dying but perhaps hopeful words, "The rest is silence" – although the gravediggers will have a lot to do.

What is *Hamlet* about?

Hamlet is a play about how a noble mind becomes unhinged – about the way in which a positive and brilliant Renaissance scholar begins to question the whole basis of the world into which he was born, turning in on himself and questioning everything in which he once believed. In showing us this so vividly it is a play which forces us, as audiences and readers, to do much as he does and to ask what, if anything, gives life value or meaning.

Hamlet has been driven into his terrible radical scepticism by the shattering events of his life. As A. C. Bradley eloquently put it in *Shakespearean Tragedy*, perhaps the most influential book ever written on the playwright, Hamlet is "already well-nigh overwhelmed with sorrow and disgust" at the beginning of the play after his father's death and his mother's "o'erhasty marriage" (in Claudius's phrase [2.2]). Then, when the Ghost appears to him, he suffers a further "tremendous shock" when he is told "that his mother was not merely what he supposed but an adulteress, and that his father was murdered by her paramour".

The terrible impact of the Ghost's "dread command" (3.4) shows in the difference between Hamlet's first and fourth soliloquies, a difference which many critics, including Bradley, disregard. But the difference is crucial if we are to understand the disintegration of Hamlet's mind.

His first soliloquy is tormented and tempestuous, with Hamlet revealing that he has only been restrained from killing himself by the divine prohibition on suicide:

> *O that this too too solid flesh would melt,*
> *Thaw and resolve itself into a dew,*
> *Or that the Everlasting had not fixed His canon*
> *gainst self-slaughter. (1.2)*

In fact, as the philosopher Schopenhauer pointed out in his famous essay "On Suicide", there is no divine prohibition on suicide in the Bible, unless we think it can be extrapolated from the sixth of the Ten Commandments: "Thou shalt not kill." But the point is that Hamlet *thinks* there is such a prohibition.

In his fourth soliloquy, Hamlet is once again "meditating on suicide", as Bradley says, but he is *not*, as Bradley also maintains, "precisely where he was at the time of his first soliloquy two months ago, before he ever heard of his father's murder". This time there is no mention of the "Everlasting", or any mention of religion whatsoever – only whether it is "nobler" simply to be a victim or to act.

> *To be, or not to be, that is the question –*
> *Whether 'tis nobler in the mind to suffer*
> *The slings and arrows of outrageous fortune,*
> *Or to take arms against a sea of troubles,*

And by opposing end them. (3.1)

This is a soliloquy distinguished by its utter
bleakness and loneliness. There is no sign here
that Hamlet is thinking about what he must do to
obey the Ghost or establish Claudius's guilt: if he is
thinking at all about the Ghost when he describes
death as "The undiscovered country from whose
bourn / No traveller returns", he certainly isn't
thinking of the Ghost as, in Bradley's phrase, a
"messenger of divine justice".

As for Claudius, there is no suggestion that, if he
is guilty, killing him could provide a remedy for the
horrors of existence that the "To be or not to be"
soliloquy so gravely, and impersonally, describes.
The whole soliloquy illustrates the French poet
Mallarmé's brilliant observation that Hamlet
makes the real world of Elsinore seem unreal, and
"effaces the too clearly defined beings about him
by the disquieting or funereal invasion of his
presence", moving through the play as "the dark
presence of the doubter".

Yet Hamlet, as we have noted, was not always
like this, and Ophelia's only soliloquy in the play is
helpful for the light it sheds on his state of mind. Her
soliloquy is concerned with the astonishing change
that has taken place in the man she loves. It is as if
there are two Hamlets, and one has disappeared:

O, what a noble mind is here o'erthrown!

The courtier's, soldier's, scholar's, eye, tongue, sword;
Th'expectancy and rose of the fair state,
The glass of fashion and the mould of form,
Th'observed of all observers – quite, quite down!
And I, of ladies most deject and wretched,
That sucked the honey of his music vow,
Now see that noble and most sovereign reason
Like sweet bells jangled out of tune and harsh;
That unmatched form and feature of blown youth
Blasted with ecstasy. O woe is me
T'have seen what I have seen, I see what I see. (3.1)

For Ophelia, the idea of two Hamlets is not some kind of metaphor. It is a terrible and inexplicable reality. But if we borrow her idea as a metaphor, we can see how her two Hamlets are both alive in the soliloquies that she can never hear, jostling and sometimes colliding with each other and very unhappily, so that their collisions produce the different kinds of logical and emotional incoherence that appear in the soliloquies.

The First Hamlet whom Ophelia recalls at such loving length had been a glorious epitome, the very embodiment of the ideal Prince and "courtier" that Christian humanist writers like Erasmus and Castiglione had imagined fondly in *The Education of a Christian Prince*(1516) and *The Book of the Courtier*(1528): a Renaissance polymath whose

Opposite: David Tennant as Hamlet and Patrick Stewart as Claudius in the RSC's 2008 production

love of the classics was always tempered by his Christian faith, a scholar who was also a soldier and was even (although the Hamlets we see onstage hardly ever make us suspect this) "the glass of fashion and the mould of form". This superman was moreover the man who, as Ophelia tells her father in vain, "hath of late made many tenders / Of his affection to me", "hath importuned me with love / In honourable fashion", and "hath given countenance to his speech, my lord, / With almost all the vows of heaven" (1.3).

The words "of late" are significant. Hamlet himself uses the same words in telling Rosencrantz and Guildenstern how he has "of late, but wherefore I know not, lost all my mirth" (2.2). But Ophelia's "of late", as well as echoing this, is helpful in a more specific way in that it confirms what has triggered her father's and brother's alarm. Hamlet has evidently been expressing love for her

RANK AND DEGREE

When Philip Larkin called his first collection of poems *The Less Deceived* he was recalling that wrenching moment in *Hamlet* when the Prince tells Ophelia, "I loved you not", and she replies: "I was the more deceived". We are unlikely to notice, and I don't think any editor mentions, her unfortunate slip, which measures her distress: she forgets to say "My lord". When Polonius dresses his daughter down so fiercely in the third

since his return from Wittenberg to attend his father's funeral – in other words, he was wooing Ophelia not long after his father's death, though not necessarily (and we might think necessarily not) after his mother's remarriage.

Not only that. As the woman Hamlet has "importuned" with "love" in "honourable fashion", Ophelia would have been the obvious person for Hamlet to confide in, had he ever wanted or needed to talk about what has shattered his life. Indeed, she was also the only available *confidante*, since Hamlet doesn't even know that Horatio is in Denmark until the end of the play's second scene. Immediately after that, in the third scene, Ophelia promises to "obey" her bullying father by cutting off all communications with Hamlet, regardless of his feelings. She keeps that promise through the next two months (between the first and second movements of the play), until her father instructs

---

scene for not "understanding" herself he means she has been forgetting her place in a feudal society and, still worse, compromising her father by forgetting his importance in the Danish hierarchy: "You do not understand yourself so clearly as it behooves my daughter, and your honour."

Hamlet himself can seem indifferent to rank and degree.

His easy and familiar welcome to the Players is characteristic and engaging. When Horatio recalls that Hamlet's father was a "goodly king", the breathtaking simplicity of Hamlet's reply is very moving:

He was a man, take him for all in all.
I shall not look upon his like again.

her to meet Hamlet again so that he and the King can eavesdrop on their conversation. Ophelia's soliloquy then confirms that Hamlet has never confided to her the reason or reasons for the terrifying change that she cannot understand.

She – or "I, of ladies most deject and wretched, / That sucked the honey of his musicked vows" (3.1) – is still helplessly bewildered by what she sees as the gulf between the man Hamlet was and the man he now is. Since she can't understand what has happened, or what has "o'erthrowne" her First Hamlet's "noble mind", the last lines of her soliloquy describe the Second Hamlet in a cursory though horrified way by emphasising that he no longer is what he was. His "noble and most sovereign reason" is now "Like sweet bells jangled, out of time and harsh", and the "unmatched form of feature of blown youth" has been "blasted with ecstasy", or madness.

Yet Hamlet's mind has *not* been completely "o'erthrown", nor has the First Hamlet died or

---

But this apparent indifference to rank and degree is not democratic, and is closely linked to what G.R. Hibbard calls Hamlet's princely hauteur. He has no scruple in pulling rank on those he dislikes or despises. Polonius, the man Hamlet describes as a "tedious old fool", has no recourse

when Hamlet bullies him into behaving like one by forcing him to agree that "yon cloud" looks like a camel, but no, wait a minute, isn't it more like a weasel, or even a whale?

Polonius has no choice but to grit however many teeth he still has and agree each time. In Act Two, scene two,

been altogether supplanted. In the tortured first soliloquy he is still fascinatingly alive, though not well. His delight in literature and his learned humanist passion for the classics still breaks through when he suddenly compares his mother's tears at his father's funeral with those of Niobe, who was "all tears" when her 14 children were killed by the gods because she loved and boasted about them too much. That reference to Niobe isn't some detachable classical allusion; it is part of the uncontrollable flood of thoughts and memories that overwhelms him when he remembers the funeral and the wedding that followed "a little month later". It is spontaneously recalled, like the marvellous detail about "those shoes": Hamlet had noticed, with characteristic keenness, how the new shoes his mother had worn for the funeral were worn again at her wedding, since too little time had passed for them to seem "old".

It's worth noticing how Niobe doesn't disappear after this characteristically rapid and unforced

---

Hamlet's behaviour is even worse: he mocks Polonius not in private but in public, telling Rosencrantz and Guildenstern that "That great baby you see there is not yet out of his swaddling clouts", and explaining to the Players that Polonius prefers "a jig or a tale of bawdry, or he sleeps".

As for the Players: having ruined their performance, Hamlet shows no concern about what may happen to them. Will they be paid, or thrown into a cell? Tom Stoppard had evidently wondered about this when he showed his Players being deported in the boat that is taking Hamlet to England. ■

reference to her being "all tears". She is still hoveringly present in the soliloquy's last lines, when Hamlet extends the contrast with his mother's "most unrighteous tears". The legendary Niobe was so inconsolable in her grief that her tears continued to flow after she had been turned into stone. Unlike Niobe's tears in this magical legend, however, Gertrude's eyes have dried too quickly.

The allusion to Niobe illustrates Ophelia's idea of there being two Hamlets, and we see this in the famous soliloquies which she can't hear. His earlier mental habits still persist, as the reflexes of a wonderfully copious and resourceful, trained mind. It is still natural to Hamlet to appeal to first principles, to recall "he who made us", and commend "god-like reason", even when he cannot keep this up. His earlier, harmonious and humanistic view of Nature has been displaced and badly shaken, but his doubts have not turned him into a nihilistic*, cynical figure like Iago – the scheming villain of Shakespeare's *Othello*.

Even the remorselessly steady anguish of the "To be or not to be" soliloquy admits his continuing concern with what is "nobler in the mind". He continues to think about "honour" more frequently than he thinks about revenge. He cannot surrender entirely the idea of honour, like Iago, Falstaff or Thersites in *Troilus and Cressida*, although he comes to wonder whether it is only "a

---

* *Nihilism is the philosophical belief that life is without meaning or intrinsic value.*

fantasy and trick of fame"[*] – and tells Rosencrantz and Guildenstern: "There is nothing either good or bad, but thinking makes it so" (2.2).

In a brilliant introduction to the New Penguin edition of *Hamlet*, Anne Barton notes: "At the end of *Richard II* (1595), Shakespeare had made it apparent that the medieval world of heraldry, honour, gages, oaths, and ceremonial combat within which the action began was now obsolete and even faintly absurd". Similarly, in *Hamlet*, says Barton, "the new reigns in Norway and Denmark appear to have closed the door on a heroic past". The contrast between Richard II and his pragmatic successor Henry IV, or between Hotspur and the Machiavellian Prince John reappear in "the distinction between the banished, chivalric world of the elder Hamlet and [King] Fortinbras and the hard-headed, unglamorous court of Claudius".

This sense of a world that has been lost – reflected in *Hamlet* and in the plays which Shakespeare wrote after *Hamlet* – is even stronger than Barton suggests. As Shakespeare was writing the play, optimism about the human condition, and the very idea of a benign universe, was being undermined in all kinds of ways. The new astronomy had decentred man as well as the planet Earth. The Italian philosopher, Machiavelli, had

* *The words come from Hamlet's seventh and last soliloquy (4.4) which appears only in the Second Quarto and was removed in the First Folio text.*

27

challenged traditional notions of degree. The French philosopher, Montaigne, had questioned natural law, our ideas of the self and just about everything else. The English metaphysical poet, John Donne, famously describes the effect of such momentous changes in his poem *The First Anniversary*, when he reflects on how "new Philosophy calls all in doubt":

> 'Tis all in pieces, all coherence gone;
> All just supply, and all Relation...

Enter Ophelia's Second Hamlet, the Hamlet whose world has been turned upside down and who can no longer believe in the world he once believed in. As the critic Philip Edwards notes, Hamlet's "To be or not to be" soliloquy represents "a trough of despair" into which we don't see

AN EPISTEMOLOGICAL TRAGEDY

Hamlet might be described as an epistemological tragedy that constantly plays on alarming gaps between what the audience knows and does not know, and between what the audience knows that characters in the play do not know. The audience knows, after listening to his attempt to pray, that Claudius did indeed murder his brother, but Hamlet never knows that. As Anne Barton rightly emphasises, "for the greater part of the play Hamlet possesses only the word of a possibly unreliable ghost, plus

Hamlet fall again – but the whole of the rest of the play is coloured by its pessimism.

And at the heart of that soliloquy, and indeed of the play itself, is a profound and disturbing quarrel about the nature of nature itself and the values we believe in. Another example of this comes at the end of the long second scene in Act Two, when Hamlet says to Rosencrantz and Guildenstern:

I have of late, but wherefore I know not, lost all my mirth, foregone all custom of exercises, and indeed it goes so heavily with my disposition that this goodly frame, the earth, seems to me a sterile promontory; this most excellent canopy the air, look you, this brave o'erhanging firmament, this majestical roof fretted with golden fire – why, it appeareth to me but a foul and pestilent congregation of vapours. What a piece of work is a man! How noble in reason, how

his own instinctive dislike of Gertrude's second husband as his basis for revenge".

Hamlet thinks he knows that Claudius killed his father, and happens to be right. But he is no less certain that Rosencrantz and Guildenstern were willing accomplices to Claudius's plan to have him murdered in England, and in that case he happens to be wrong – or, at the very least, has no solid grounds for his belief that Rosencrantz and Guildenstern are aware of the contents of the sealed letter (ordering Hamlet's death) that they are to deliver to the King of England.

Neither Hamlet nor the audience ever know the extent of Gertrude's guilt, although Hamlet thinks he knows that too when he says "almost as bad good mother, / As kill a king, and marry with his brother".

infinite in faculties, in form and moving, how express and admirable, in action how like an angel, in apprehension how like a god! The beauty of the world, the paragon of the animals – and yet, what is this quintessence of dust? Man delights not me...

It is a speech often seen as, in Philip Edwards's words, "a brilliant perception of the anguish of Renaissance man in general and of Hamlet in particular". But at the end of the speech Hamlet punctures the rhetoric himself – "Man delights not me" – and there is little in the play to lighten his dark view of the human condition. *Hamlet* may keep open, just, the "possibility", as Edwards puts it, that "there is a higher court of values" than those which operate around us and that the words "salvation" and "damnation" have meaning, but it seems, by the time we have witnessed the horrors of the last act, a very faint possibility.

Hamlet is devastated by the Ghost's claim that Claudius had "Won to his shameful lust / The will of my most seeming virtuous queen". Yet neither we nor Hamlet can know whether Claudius had, as Hamlet puts it, "whored my mother" weeks or months or even years before he "killed my king". By the end of the closet scene we cannot even be sure that Gertrude herself knows that her second husband killed King Hamlet – just as we can never be certain whether Ophelia knows or even suspects that Prince Hamlet killed her father.

While we know that Hamlet has seen the Ghost, Claudius never knows or suspects this. And in the final scenes does

Who or what is the Ghost?

Whenever Christianity enters Shakespearean tragedy it is usually as a source of further terror, not consolation. *Hamlet* seems to me no exception to this general rule. From the moment we hear about the Ghost in the first scene, Shakespeare is raising questions about the nature of Christianity. What is the Ghost? Where does it come from? What does it want?

In Act One, Scene Five, Hamlet asks precisely this in his astounded and fearful response when he first sees the Ghost:

> *Angels and ministers of grace defend us!*
> *Be thou a spirit of health, or goblin damned,*
> *Bring with thee airs from heaven or blasts from hell,*
> *Be thy intents wicked or charitable,*
> *Thou com'st in such a questionable shape*
> *That I will speak to thee. (1.5)*

Gertrude insist on drinking because she suspects the wine is poisoned and intended for Hamlet? We can never know, because the text does not tell us, what happens between Gertrude and Claudius, from the moment when she promises to her son that she will stop sleeping with her husband to the moment when she places herself between Claudius and Laertes's sword – just as we can never know what happens to Hamlet that might account for the difference between his almost jubilant mood at the end of Act Two and his profoundly discouraged mood, shortly afterwards, when he delivers his most famous soliloquy. ∎

To Professor Roy Battenhouse, a deeply Christian critic, the question Hamlet poses to himself about the Ghost's intentions is the most important of all the questions to be answered about the play (see p.41). And when Battenhouse says that Hamlet doesn't pursue or answer it, he means that he never pursues it in any sustained or rigorous way, and that the answers he does give are wildly different. This is certainly true.

At the end of Act One, when Hamlet rejoins Horatio and the others after his meeting with the Ghost, he declares: "It is an honest ghost, that let me tell you." Moments later, however, when Horatio and the others hear the Ghost speaking for the first time, Hamlet addresses "this fellow in the cellarage" in a familiar and even mocking way, calling it "boy", "truepenny" and "old mole", as though it were another of the stage devils that inhabited or disappeared into the "cellarage" under the Elizabethan platform stage.

In the "Oh what a rogue and peasant slave" soliloquy at the end of Act Two, his doubts are troubling him again, and he is considering whether the Ghost was sent to take advantage of his suicidal melancholy:

> *The spirit that I have seen*
> *May be the devil – and the devil hath power*
> *T'assume a pleasing shape. Yea, and perhaps,*
> *Out of my weakness and my melancholy,*

As he is very potent with such spirits,
Abuses me to damn me. I'll have grounds
More relative than this. (2.2)

He then plans to set the "Mousetrap" – as a way of testing the Ghost as well as Claudius. In the two months that have passed since he heard its "dread command", he has done nothing. Now, his spirits seem to lift as he makes his ingenious plan. But then – not many minutes later in the theatre, and on the very next morning in the play's timeline – he is delivering his "To be or not to be" soliloquy and describing death as a country from which "no traveller returns". He can hardly have forgotten the Ghost, but at this point, with the Mousetrap only hours away, he seems, once again, to have rejected the idea that the Ghost could be what it claimed to be: "thy father's spirit".

Then – finally – when he thinks that the Mousetrap has been a complete success, he tells Horatio: "I'll take the ghost's word for a thousand pound" (3.2). And after this he never again worries about whether the Ghost might be "a goblin damn'd", not "a spirit of health", whether it comes "from heaven" or "from hell", and whether its intentions might be "wicked" not "charitable". He stops thinking about the most important question, or three questions, that he himself had posed as soon as he saw the Ghost.

So when the Ghost makes its final appearance

in the so-called closet scene – and not in its suit of armour but in a "nightgown", according to the First Quarto – the guilt-stricken Hamlet asks, "What would your gracious figure?" and refers to himself as "your tardy son":

> *Do you not come your tardy son to chide,*
> *That lapsed in time and passion lets go by*
> *Th'important acting of your dread command? (3.4)*

By this time, nothing can shake Hamlet's belief that the Ghost just is what from the first it claimed to be – "thy father's spirit".

It is not surprising, then, that this is how the Ghost was regarded throughout the long tradition of seeing the play through Hamlet's eyes. Nineteenth-century critics speculated endlessly about the possible reasons for Hamlet's "delay" without ever considering that one very strong and grave reason for not sweeping to his revenge was Hamlet's doubts about the Ghost's provenance. In this respect Bradley's view that the Ghost is not only the ghost of Hamlet's father but the "majestic" and incontrovertible "messenger of divine justice" is the apotheosis of this entrenched tradition.

Indeed Bradley goes further, arguing that *Hamlet* can be seen as Shakespeare's "most religious" play and making light of all Hamlet's doubts about the Ghost. So Hamlet's troubled lines about how the Ghost "may be a devil", for example, are dismissed as "an unconscious fiction" and an "excuse":

> Evidently this sudden doubt, of which there has not been the slightest trace before, is no genuine doubt; it is an unconscious fiction, an excuse for his delay – and its continuance.

Sudden? Not the slightest trace before? This is quite astonishing, and cannot be explained as a mere lapse of memory. Bradley, the most celebrated of all Shakespeare critics, is normally so lovingly respectful of the text, which he could probably have reconstructed from memory. He could hardly have forgotten what Hamlet said when he first saw the Ghost. Rather, he has blocked it out, because he is so convinced that Hamlet should have obeyed the Ghost's "dread command":

> Hamlet, it is impossible to deny, habitually assumes, without any questioning, that he ought to avenge his father.

Bradley goes on:

> Surely it is clear that, whatever we in the twentieth century may think about Hamlet's delay, we are meant in the play to assume that he ought to have obeyed the Ghost.

But it isn't at all clear, as we have seen, though Bradley is by no means the only important Shakespeare critic to take the Ghost at his word.

Stephen Greenblatt writes in *Hamlet in Purgatory* that

> [t]he closet scene is the last time that Hamlet – or the audience – sees the spirit of his father". Like Bradley, Greenblatt assumes that the Ghost just is the spirit of Hamlet's father.

Others, however, are more sceptical – and they are surely right to be. Perhaps John Dover Wilson's greatest achievement in *What Happens in Hamlet?* (1935) was to show how the doubts about the Ghost's provenance would have been very real and alarming to the play's first audiences. No less importantly, Dover Wilson argued that Shakespeare constructs his play "so carefully that we are never perfectly certain as to just who or what the Ghost is":

> Hamlet is given a mandate that he cannot ignore, but from a source which remains mysterious from first to last.

Why are the doubts about the Ghost so disturbing?

When the American critic Stephen Greenblatt set out to write his book *Hamlet in Purgatory*, he was concerned, he says, only with the "poetics" of Purgatory; his "goal was not to understand the theology behind the ghost; still less, to determine whether it was 'Catholic' or 'Protestant'... My only goal was to immerse myself in the tragedy's magical intensity." This is rather like being concerned with the "poetics" and "magical intensity" of a torture chamber, rather than with what it actually is.

I think Wittgenstein was right to argue, in his *Lectures on Aesthetics*, that we cannot usefully discuss "poetics" – or so-called aesthetic values – without being concerned with the subject matter behind them. In other words, the constant emphasis on "poetics" in Greenblatt's *Hamlet in Purgatory* sets it strangely apart from the historical, once-lived realities that fuelled what we might call the "*Hamlet*-terror" – the frightening dilemma into which the Ghost plunges Hamlet.

To diminish this play's religious terrors is to diminish its dramatic terrors. Whether or not we agree with A.C. Bradley that this is Shakespeare's most religious play, religion is at the centre of it, and of what we make of the Ghost's instructions to Hamlet.

The Ghost, we must remember, sets him two tasks, not one. He must kill Claudius; this is, at best, the Old Testament view of revenge at its most primitive. But Hamlet is also told he must not "taint" his mind, and must leave his mother "to heaven" and to those thorns that in her bosom lodge "to prick and sting" her: this invokes the New Testament ethic, with its emphasis on inner repentance and its absolute prohibition of revenge.

A better introduction to *Hamlet* than Greenblatt's study might be the poem, *Satyre III: Of Religion*, by the metaphysical poet, John Donne. *Satyre III* is a plea for tolerance in the divided, intolerant world of the 1590s, in which Protestants and Catholics denounced each other and Catholics were systematically persecuted.

It would be fatuous to suppose that *Hamlet* will tell us where Shakespeare's sympathies lay, whether he accepted or rejected Protestant teaching on purgatory (Protestants argued that there was no such thing), whether he saw the Ghost as an instrument of Heaven or a "goblin damn'd" or indeed whether or not he actually believed in God. What can be said is that in his lifetime, when science did not offer any alternative account of creation to that presented by the Christian doctrine, most people thought it crazy to deny the existence of a Creator. How else could one account for the existence of everything else – that did exist?

There were atheists, of course, though they kept quiet about what they believed or refused to believe. To declare yourself one was like committing suicide: you would be killed, and your family left penniless, as well as disgraced. And the machinery of State and ecclesiastical censorship ensured that no "atheistic" book could ever be published. Christopher Marlowe, the dramatist who most influenced young Shakespeare, was widely believed to be an atheist and belonged to the sinister-sounding "School of Night", also known as the "School of Atheism" (centred, it is believed, round Sir Walter Raleigh).

In Shakespeare's plays the atheists are usually, but not always, villains like Edmund in *King Lear* or Iago in *Othello*. The non-villainous exceptions, like Claudio in *Measure for Measure*, are more startling. Claudio has been sentenced to death "for getting a maid with child"; the reasons why Claudio and the heavily pregnant Julietta haven't married don't matter here. What matters is that Claudio and Julietta are the only mutually loving couple in that very dark comedy, and that the decent, instructively ordinary Claudio plainly doesn't believe in the Christian account of what happens after death when he launches into his terrified speech, "Ay, but to die, and go we know not where..."*

* *Many more atheists came to light in the next century when, for a few brief years, censorship was abolished by Oliver Cromwell. Cromwell himself was appalled when he saw what even some of his soldiers believed: there is no Heaven but women, one declared, and no Hell but marriage. Of course censorship was restored even before the new King returned in 1660.*

Whether Shakespeare was an atheist we don't know. Donne certainly was not: he was ordained as a Protestant and eventually became Dean of St Paul's. But his poem *Satyre III* is a scornful indictment of the religious terrorism of the 1590s. He hated intolerance, maintaining both before and after his ordination that in "all Christian professions there is a way to salvation". Though it couldn't be published, *Satyre III* circulated privately, and Shakespeare may have acquired a copy from the playwright Ben Jonson, a friend of his as well as of Donne. It would be astonishing if Shakespeare hadn't read it before he wrote *Hamlet*. Donne's *Satyre III* provides a better introduction to *Hamlet* than Greenblatt's study because it helps us to relate what happens in the play to the terrors faced by all those who struggled with the problem of authority in the intolerant world of the 1590s. Indeed, if we take *Satyre III* as a guide to that world and its presence in *Hamlet*, we might go further. Even after his ordination, Donne feared that the rival religions might – by misrepresenting the moral nature of God – drive men into disbelief. If we were looking for a great work in which Donne's fear was realised, we might consider *Hamlet* – where, if we "take the Ghost's word", divine justice would appear to have the morals of a fruit machine.

The idea that even the best of men must burn in hellish or purgatorial fires if they have the bad luck to die unanointed is itself barbaric; yet this is the reason for the torments the Ghost says he suffers. The idea resurfaces as Hamlet's reason for not slaughtering the King while he is at prayer – he believes the King won't go to hell if he kills him in this state.

Nor does Hamlet, despite his eloquence and the power and subtlety of his mind, ever ask the obviously pressing question about the ethics of revenge. To put it brutally, he never questions the moral nature of a deity who will fry his father for allowing himself to be murdered before he had engaged a priest. If *Hamlet* did not raise questions in an Elizabethan audience about the existence of God, it undoubtedly raised them about just how benevolent that God might be.

Ears

King Hamlet is murdered by having poison poured in his ear. The great French critic Hippolyte Taine says the play is also "the story of a moral poisoning" – the Ghost pours a more excruciating poison into young Hamlet's ear when it claims that the Queen was sleeping with both brothers before one killed the other.

Ears feature prominently in *Hamlet*. Here are some examples:

And let us once again assail your ears,
They are fortified against our story (1.1)

....

Nor shall you do my ear that violence
To make it truster of your own report (1.2)

....

But this eternal blazon must not be
To ears of flesh and blood (1.5)

....

So the whole ear of Denmark
Is by a forged process of my death
Rankly abused (1.5)

....

and with a hideous crash

Take prisoner Pyrrhus' ear (2.2)

....

And I'll be placed, so please you, in the ear

Of all their conference (3.1)

....

And wants not buzzers to infect his ear

With pestilent speeches...(4.4)

....

I have words to speak in thine ear will make thee dumb (4.4)

....

We can be mistaken "in what we see", says Tony Tanner in his introduction to the Everyman *Hamlet*, "and we can hallucinate". We can be mistaken in what we touch, too, or in identifying a taste or smell. "But in no other sense are we so vulnerable as in our hearing." Tanner quotes Montaigne – our ears "are the most dangerous instruments we have to receive violent and sudden impressions to trouble and alter us" – and, agreeing with Hippolyte Taine, says that the Ghost "poisons" Hamlet's ear with the truth of murder and incest – "for there are truths which, to all intents and purposes, 'poison' the hearer".

How important is Gertrude's incest?

Is Hamlet more horrified by his mother's incestuous remarriage than by the Ghost's shattering revelation, or claim, that Gertrude was sleeping with both brothers before one killed the other? I think that he is far more horrified by his mother's adultery than by her incest, but a number of important 20th century critics think otherwise, believing the question of incest to be crucial.

In *What Happens in 'Hamlet'* (1944), John Dover Wilson insists:

> No one can doubt for one moment that Shakespeare wished... to make full dramatic capital out of Gertrude's infringement of ecclesiastical law, and expected his audience to look upon it with as much abhorrence as the Athenians felt [for Oedipus's] crime.

Similarly, the Freudian critic Ernest Jones insists in *Hamlet and Oedipus* (1949) that there can be "no question" of "the profound difference in Hamlet's attitude" towards "Claudius's incest with the Queen, and his murder of his brother... Intellectually of course he abhors both, but there can be no question as to which arouses in him the deeper loathing" – namely, the incest. We might have to agree about that if it explained what turns Hamlet into a man who, as A.D. Nuttall bluntly puts it in *Shakespeare the Thinker*, is "incapable, seemingly, of a normal sexual relationship with a loving woman". But it does not explain that. As we have seen, Hamlet was wooing Ophelia after his return from Wittenberg for his father's funeral. There is no sign whatever of the extraordinary and disabling horror of sex, or sex nausea, that erupts in his tirades against Ophelia and his mother until he has met the questionable Ghost at the end of Act One.

As Nuttall observes, it is only once he has met the Ghost – and been told that his father was murdered by his uncle – that the "young, ordinarily likable Hamlet" we glimpse in the letter to Ophelia ("O dear Ophelia, I am ill at these numbers" [2.2]) becomes a man "from whom all ordinary, human natural relationships have been withdrawn". For Nuttall, this later shock was even more unendurable than the earlier shock of his mother's remarriage. The later shock, says Nuttall, is what separates Hamlet "from the sustaining link with continuing life" so that his "motivation decays".

Our view of how much incest matters in the play depends on whether we believe Nuttall, on the one hand, or Dover Wilson and Ernest Jones on the other.

While Gertrude's second marriage to her brother-in-law is not incestuous under modern

English law, it certainly was under Elizabethan law. The 1567 Incest Act made it clear that to marry or fornicate with your dead husband's brother or dead wife's sister was every bit as "abhominabill vile and filthie" as marrying or having sex with your natural brother or sister. The Act was based on "Goddis word" – as drawn from the 18th chapter of Leviticus – and this was taken to be timeless and eternal and binding on all future ages, cultures and societies.

But the fact that incest was illegal does not explain why some modern critics have found Gertrude's marriage so disturbing. As A.J.A. Waldock suggests as early as 1931, in his

GERTRUDE

"The singular thing about Gertrude is that nothing happens to her. She dies by accident, of a sudden thirst, and is allowed just enough breath to swell the scene and inflame further the passion of her son... [We] are left no sense of a change, or a choice, having occurred in Gertrude's life. Shakespeare offers no hint of a then/now contrast (as he does with Hamlet) or no "aside" in which her truth is permitted to surface (as he does with Claudius); all we are told is that in the old days her love for King Hamlet seemed to grow by what it fed on and in the present she is, to all appearances, complacently – if not devotedly – married to his brother to whom she was, in a sense, passed on."

From Hamlet and the Concept of Character *by Bert O. States* ∎

profoundly thoughtful *Hamlet: A Study in Critical Method,* the obsession with incest undoubtedly owed a good deal to Freud. Before Freud, no critic had attended so closely to the play's "sexual quality" and Hamlet's sex nausea, or to his obsession with what he imagines goes on between his mother and Claudius

> *In the rank sweat of an enseamed bed.*
> *Stewed in corruption, honeying and making love*
> *Over the nasty sty. (3.4)*

Dover Wilson believed that all Elizabethans, including Shakespeare, would have regarded Gertrude's second marriage as "abhorrent". But there is no evidence that Elizabethans really believed that marrying a brother-in-law was as "abhominable vile and filthy" as marrying a brother – only that the State and the Church, through the 1567 Incest Act, wanted them to think that way.

The second problem with Dover Wilson's argument is that the only two characters in *Hamlet* who refer to Gertrude's second marriage as incestuous are the Ghost and Hamlet. The others are all silent or acquiescent on the matter. Dover Wilson sees this as a measure of their corruption. Yet both Horatio and Ophelia are unquestionably decent, not corrupt. Horatio never mentions the incest at all, although his comment on how the marriage "followed hard upon" the funeral shows that he thinks that Gertrude should have mourned her first husband for longer: mourning for longer, however, couldn't have improved matters if her remarriage were really "filthie".

As for Ophelia, we might think that it wouldn't be characteristic of her to comment on this matter, even if the legally or technically incestuous nature of Gertrude's second marriage filled her with the horror and loathing Dover Wilson insists Shakespeare "expected his audience to feel". But if that was what Ophelia felt she would never have been as puzzled as she is in her soliloquy by the question of what had "o'erthrowne" Hamlet's "noble mind".

Rather ironically, the two incestuous sinners are both silent on this matter on the two occasions when we might expect them to mention it. In Act Two, scene two, when Polonius comes up with his new theory that frustrated love for Ophelia is the "very cause of Hamlet's lunacy", Claudius takes this more seriously than Gertrude. Once Polonius has left them alone, she reminds her husband of what she takes to be the "main" cause:

I doubt it is no other but the main:
His father's death, and our o'erhasty marriage. (2.2)

Although they are now talking quietly and

confidentially between themselves, Gertrude doesn't mention the matter of incest as something that might have contributed to Hamlet's disturbance. Nor does Claudius in his "Oh my offence is rank" soliloquy in Act Three, scene three, when he is trying to pray. He confesses, with profound horror, the sin of "a brother's murder" that "smells to heaven" and "hath the primal eldest curse upon't". But he never mentions the matter of incest.

So what of Hamlet? A. C. Bradley notes that Hamlet refers to incest "three" times, with the first such reference coming near the end of his first soliloquy: "Oh most wicked speed, to post / With such dexterity to incestuous sheets" (1.2). Yet this reference to incest seems curiously weightless. Until this moment, and even through most of the sentence in question, Hamlet has been in anguish about the "speed" with which his mother could marry again, "within a month": "O God, a beast that wants discourse of reason / Would have mourned longer" (1.2). He is devastated not so much by the nature of the marriage his mother is contemplating as by his mother's failure to mourn for longer.

The same inconsequentiality reappears in Hamlet's "Now might I do it pat" soliloquy when he determines that he can best ensure Claudius's damnation by not killing him now when he is praying but

> *When he is drunk asleep, or in his rage,*
> *Or in th'incestuous pleasure of his bed,*
> *At gaming, swearing, or about some act*
> *That hath no relish of salvation in't... (3.3)*

That puts incest on a par with swearing or gambling or being "in rage" – which could then mean being in a state of uncontrollable sexual desire. And yet, if Claudius's marriage to his sister-in law were as incestuous and "abhominabill vile and filthie" as marrying a real sister there would be no need whatever for Hamlet to wait until Claudius is enjoying himself in bed: whenever he is killed or dies, he would almost certainly be damned.

Hamlet's next references to incest, or at least to Gertrude's having married her dead husband's brother, come when he confronts his mother in the closet scene.* Early on, Hamlet says to his mother: "You are the queen, your husband's brother's wife" (3.4). G.R. Hibbard, the editor of the New Cambridge edition of the play, explains that here Hamlet "is accusing his mother of incest". This may be so, yet if it is the accusation is surprisingly understated, and Gertrude herself shows no sign of taking it in. A more heated exchange follows a few moments later, when Hamlet has killed Polonius and Gertrude exclaims: "O what a rash and bloody deed is this!" Hamlet replies:

---

* *The last time Hamlet uses the word is when he kills Claudius in the last scene, calling him "thou incestuous, murderous, damned Dane..."*

A bloody deed – almost as bad, good mother,
As kill a king and marry with his brother.

To which the astonished Gertrude replies, "As kill a King?" – while ignoring the second charge. If the actor playing Hamlet tries to keep it in view by leaning on the word "brother" each time, Gertrude's complete silence on this matter is all the more striking. When Gertrude asks

What have I done, that thou dar'st wag they tongue
In noise so rude against me?

Hamlet's lengthy, furious but unspecific reply doesn't make any explicit reference to incest, although G.R. Hibbard says Hamlet's thundering "Such an act" means "adultery joined to incest".

INCEST AND CHRISTIAN CULTURE

In other Christian countries and cultures, "Goddis Word" was interpreted differently when it came to incest. So, for example, marrying your dead husband's brother was encouraged in some Asian countries like Japan, especially in times of war, and was required in many African tribes like the Yoruba, Igbo and Tiv in Nigeria.

In a fascinating essay on "Shakespeare in the Bush", Laura Bohannen recalls how the Tiv elders cried out "He did well", when she told them how, in the story of Hamlet, Claudius married his sister-in-law. To return closer to home: among those Elizabethan men and the smaller number of

There is no sign, however, that Gertrude *herself* understands that this is what her son means by "Such an act". Indeed, even by the end of this lacerating scene we cannot be sure that she understands that her first husband was killed by the second. At this point, when her son still isn't answering her question "What have I done?", she interrupts him by asking, once again and with understandable desperation, *what act* is in question:

> *Ay me, what act,*
> *That roars so loud and thunders in the index...* (3.4)

Philip Edwards, who takes a very different view to Hibbard, notes:

> When Gertrude directly asks him "what

women who could read, and read their Bibles, some would have noticed and perhaps been puzzled by the apparent contradiction between what "Goddis Word" prohibits in Leviticus and mandates in Deuteronomy 25.5:

> If brethren dwell together, and one of them die, and have no child, the wife of the dead shall not marry without unto a stranger: her husband's brother shall go in unto her, and take her to him to wife, and perform the duty of an husband's brother unto her.

In English law, no widow in Gertrude's situation was free to marry her deceased husband's brother until the 1907 Marriage Act, and it didn't become legal for a divorced woman to marry her ex-husband's brother until 1960. In Scotland, the incest laws were not fully relaxed until 1986. ∎

act?", he does not directly answer "adultery", but charges her with inconstancy, immoderate sexual desire, and a lack of any sense of value in exchanging King Hamlet for Claudius. He does not pursue the charge of adultery, but nothing he says shows him forgetting it.

So what of the Ghost's two references to the marriage as "incestuous"? The Ghost first refers to Claudius as "that incestuous, that adulterate beast" who "won to his shameful lust / The will of my most seeming-virtuous queen", and later tells Hamlet not to let "the royal bed of Denmark be / A couch for luxury and damnèd incest" (1.5).

The first reference clearly implies that Gertrude and Claudius were lovers before Claudius murdered old King Hamlet. What torments Hamlet – from his first soliloquy to the final scene, where he refers to Claudius as the man who "killed my King, and whored my mother" – is not the idea that her re-marriage was "incestuous", but the thought that his mother was "adulterate" and was sleeping with both brothers before one killed the other. That terrible suspicion or fear is already pressing in the first soliloquy, before he meets the Ghost, and that surely is what haunts him more than any thoughts of incest.

Does Hamlet suffer from an Oedipus Complex?

Hamlet became the crippled patron saint of Freudian psychoanalysis in 1897, when Freud wrote to his friend and fellow-analyst Wilhelm Fliess to say how he had arrived at his new theory of the Oedipus Complex by thinking about the old problem in *Hamlet*. How was Hamlet's delay in avenging his father's murder to be explained? "How better," wrote Freud, "than through the torment he suffers from the obscure memory that he himself had contemplated the same deed against his father out of passion for his mother."

In a brilliant essay on "Freud and Shakespeare: Hamlet", A.D. Nuttall provided this admirably laconic summary of Freud's grandly inclusive theory:

All male children pass through a phase in which they wish to murder their fathers and have sexual intercourse with their mothers. We have grown accustomed to Freud's famous theory of the Oedipus Complex. The simple sentence in which the theory is stated no longer shocks. Does this mean that we have learned to accept the proposition as true? If we have indeed reached a stage of belief – as distinct from mere numb habituation – then, I suggest, we ought not to have done so. There might indeed be something salutary in using our imagination to recover the original shock effect. The shock arose not only from the sexual content of the sentence but also from sheer implausibility. If ever a statement needed to earn acceptance by vigorous demonstration, it was this.

Nuttall then wryly recalled how "the philosopher Sidney Hook asked one psychoanalyst after another what would count as evidence that a child had not got an Oedipus Complex, and never obtained an answer".

Nuttall's point was that the Freudian theory was only *quasi*– or *pseudo*-scientific, since it was not

IS HAMLET MAD?

"Hamlet is idiotically insane," wrote the librettist W.S. Gilbert. "With lucid intervals of lunacy." The name Amleth derives from the Old Norse for an idiot, or for someone who feigns idiocy. In the original Danish chronicle by Saxo Grammaticus, Prince Amleth is in real danger from his murderous uncle and cunningly pretends to be mad to preserve his life. There is no evidence that Shakespeare departed from this in his play.

Significantly, Rosencrantz and Guildenstern never believe he is mad. He tells them himself that he is "but mad north-north-west" – when the wind is southerly, he can tell "a hawk from a handsaw" (2.2) – and Guildenstern talks of his use of "crafty madness" (3.1) to lead them astray. Claudius claims that Hamlet is mad, but only because he needs an

falsifiable or open to contrary evidence in the way that any genuinely scientific theory or thesis is, according to the philosopher Karl Popper's principle of "falsifiability". Wittgenstein similarly protested that Freud's method of argument depended on persuasion, not evidence; another case in point was Freud's notorious argument that no woman can resist rape with her full strength.

Hamlet's frequent and moving expressions of love for his dead father are thus construed as evidence of how hard he is struggling to repress his real wishes. The Oedipus Complex, according to Freud's theory, dates from the "phallic stage" of psychological development when a child is three and four – so Freud had good reason to tell Fliess

excuse to be rid of him, while Gertrude says he is "Mad as the sea and wind, when both contend", but only because she wants to excuse his murder of Polonius. And while Ophelia gives a graphic description of his distracted behaviour in Act Two, scene one, this comes immediately after Hamlet himself has told Horatio and Marcellus at the end of Act One that he will put on an "antic disposition" to disguise what he is up to.

Plenty of actors have played Hamlet as mad, or intermittently mad, while others, like Laurence Olivier in the 1948 film, play him as entirely sane. When characters are really mad in Shakespeare's plays, they tend to speak in prose, as Lear does after he is driven demented by the sight of Edgar. Ophelia herself mixes prose with songs when she goes mad before her death at the end of Act Four. There is nothing mad about Hamlet's actions in the final act of the play, and his use of madness as an excuse to explain his behaviour to Laertes seems no more than an excuse. ∎

TEN FACTS ABOUT
HAMLET

1.

Running to 4,042 lines and 29,551 words, *Hamlet* is Shakespeare's longest play and takes more than four hours to perform, uncut. It has only been dramatised in its entirety on film once – by Kenneth Branagh in 1996.

2.

The first actor to play Hamlet , in around 1601, was Richard Burbage, the lead actor in Shakespeare's company, The King's Men.

3.

The story of Hamlet ultimately derives from the Danish legend of Amleth, as recounted by the 13th century chronicler, Saxo Grammaticus. Shake-speare is also thought to have drawn on an earlier Elizabethan play about Hamlet, which may have been written by Thomas Kyd in or before 1589 (though some scholars believe it was an early work by Shakespeare himself).

4.

As Jan Kott observed in his seminal *Shakespeare Our Contemporary*, Hamlet is one of the few characters who lives not only beyond the text of the play but also beyond theatre. The Polish poet, Zbigniew Herbert, for example, wrote an "Ode of Fortinbras", while one of Dr Zhivago's poems in Boris Pasternak's novel is called "Hamlet" and ends with the line: "To live life is not to cross a field."

5.

Shakespeare's only son, Hamnet, died in 1596, aged 11. James Joyce was the first to suggest that this had a strong influence on the play, though a number of critics have since argued that the co-incidence of names cannot be ignored and that Shakespeare's grief about his son's death may have inspired *Hamlet*.

6.

The American critic Harold Bloom believes that only one Shakepearean character, Sir John Falstaff, can rival Hamlet " in comprehensiveness of consciousness and keenness of intellect". Hamlet and Falstaff are central to Bloom's contention that Shakespeare invented "the human": that the very way we now think about ourselves – the whole concept of personality as we now understand it – is due to Shakespeare.

7.

In the Royal Shakespeare Company production of Hamlet in 2008, David Tennant used a real skull as a prop in the gravedigger scene. The skull had belonged to the composer André Tchaikowsky who bequeathed it to the RSC when he died in 1982 "for use in theatrical performance".

8.

A hundred years after Shakespeare's death the writer Nicholas Rowe reported that he had heard that Shakespeare himself played the Ghost at the Globe, though there is no evidence to support this.

9.

Hamlet is said to be the second most filmed story in the world, after Cinderella. There have been more than 50 screen adaptations since the first black and white film of the play in 1908.

10.

In "Hamlet Made Simple", David P. Gontar turns the tables on the psychoanalyst critics like Freud by suggesting that Claudius is actually Prince Hamlet's real, biological father. It is this, argues Gontar, which explains his unwillingness to kill him.

Opposite: David Warner as Hamlet and Estelle Kohler as Ophelia in Peter Hall's 1965 production at the Royal Shakespeare theatre

that Hamlet's own memory of this would have been "obscure".

The critic Ernest Jones – a disciple of Freud's – speculates (as Freud himself does) that Shakespeare *himself* was suffering from a repressed but reactivated Oedipal process which made him unconscious of "what the play projects", and that those who oppose the Freudian theory are similarly repressed.

It will already be clear, however, that I agree with René Girard's conclusion in *Violence and the Sacred* (1972) that we should "cast off that most burdensome of all mythologies: the myth of the Oedipus Complex".

Freud's claims about Shakespeare and Hamlet are hard to take seriously. As if in recognition of the difficulty of proof, Freud himself emphasised that his theory penetrated to "the deepest stratum of the mind of the creative poet". And since it suited his theory so well, he was happy to avail himself of the Danish critic Georg Brandes's argument that *Hamlet* was written with truly amazing speed after Shakespeare's father died in September 1601.

Are Rosencrantz and Guildenstern "excellent good friends" – or "adders fang'd"?

In *An Actor and His Time* (1979) John Gielgud – discussing an American film of *Hamlet* he made with Richard Burton – wrote dismissively about some of Shakespeare's minor characters:

> In Shakespeare's plays, characters like Rosencrantz and Guildenstern, Salarino, and all those lords in the historical plays, are not developed individually, but can be turned into effective cameos if clever actors play them. In America I was attacked after every rehearsal by desperate actors, asking "What is this character about?" I fear that, in the end, my ill-tempered reply would be "It's about being a good feed for Hamlet."

The idea that characters like Rosencrantz and Guildenstern are chiefly there to be "a good feed for Hamlet" is another consequence of the tradition of seeing the play through Hamlet's eyes. In *Five and Eighty Hamlets*, the veteran reviewer J. C. Trewin said that theatrical people would often refer to Rosencrantz and Guildenstern as "the Knife and Fork". The same idea explains the old theatrical joke that when Claudius welcomes them to Denmark he can't even remember which of them is which, so that Gertrude has to correct him.

Both Richard Burton and John Gielgud explained in interviews that Hamlet could never have regarded them as real friends. As Burton scornfully put it, "I can only think they were very nodding acquaintances, Rosencrantz and Guildenstern doing most of the nodding". Gielgud also thought that "One doesn't quite see those two, with Horatio and Hamlet, having a midnight binge" – though it's hard to imagine Hamlet and Horatio having a midnight binge with or without the hapless pair. More significantly, Gielgud added that Rosencrantz and Guildenstern are "horrid creatures, really – just toadies to the King. All the people round Hamlet are very second-rate, and Hamlet loathes second-rate things."

The tradition of playing Rosencrantz and Guildenstern as an undistinguished and barely distinguishable brace of toadies, however, is awkwardly at odds with the evident pleasure Hamlet shows when he first sees them. He seems happily surprised, exclaiming: "My excellent good friends! How dost thou, Guildenstern? Ah, Rosencrantz. Good lads, how do you both?" (2.2). His warmly affectionate greeting bears out the Queen's certainty that her son would be delighted to see his old schoolfellows again. As she told the Knife and the Fork when she welcomed them to Denmark:

Good gentlemen, he hath much talked of you,
And sure I am, two men there is not living
To whom he more adheres. (2.2)

When the Queen says this she still knows nothing
of Horatio, the friend to whom Hamlet most
"adheres", and there is no good reason to doubt
what she says about Hamlet's declared fondness
for these earlier companions.

The no-less-welcoming Claudius, who likes to
put everyone at their ease, explains at once how
"The need we have to use you did provoke / Our
hasty sending":

Something have you heard
Of Hamlet's transformation – so call it,
Sith nor th'exterior nor the inward man
Resembles that it was. What it should be,
More than his father's death, that thus hath put him
So much from th'understanding of himself,
I cannot dream of.

Two months have passed since Hamlet was so
publicly hostile to Claudius in the play's second
scene, before he had met the Ghost. In that time he
has done nothing about the Ghost's "dread
command", except feign madness and think. His
"transformation" (as Claudius calls it) or "lunacy"
(as Polonius calls it), has evidently become a
matter of such general concern and gossip that the

King assumes Rosencrantz and Guildenstern will have heard already. From their point of view, this genial but concerned king is simply setting his cards upon the table when he explains why he wants to "use" them.

They both readily agree to that, and the Queen says "amen" to Guildenstern's elegantly ceremonious little prayer that they can be of help to their old friend and to Denmark:

> *Heavens make our presence and our practices*
> *Pleasant and helpful to him.*

As G.K. Hunter and Philip Edwards both note in their excellent editions of the play, Rosencrantz's word "practices" refers to their imminent "doings" and "activities". Edwards adds that the word was also "very frequently used to mean a stratagem, or underhand scheme", and so it was, but Hamlet's loving mother would not be giving her "amen" if she thought Rosencrantz and Guildenstern were planning something underhand.

Indeed, Hamlet's old friends have no reason whatever to suspect that they might be being engaged as spies, just as Claudius himself has no reason to fear that Hamlet could possibly know that his father was murdered. Later, Claudius might very well wish that he had let his new and difficult son return to Wittenberg, but when he and the Queen press Hamlet to stay in Denmark they

Jamie Parker as Guildenstern and Samuel Barnett as Rosencrantz in Tom Stoppard's play Rosencrantz and Guildenstern are Dead

have good reason to think that the deeply depressed Hamlet might be suicidal, as Hamlet's first soliloquy confirms.

Whether we find Rosencrantz and Guildenstern engaging and amusing in the first stage of the reunion will depend, in the theatre, on whether Hamlet enjoys it. The initial, student-like banter (which Hamlet starts) about the strumpet Fortune's "secret" parts won't seem enjoyable if the Hamlet is as cool and narrow-eyed as Richard Burton's Hamlet, who points at them and sneers as soon as they laugh at one of his jokes. David Warner as the Student Prince showed in Peter Hall's 1965 production, however, that the reunion can be happy enough – until Hamlet asks, in a seemingly casual way, "what make you at Elsinore?"

This immediately puts his old friends on the spot, not because they are spies or enemies or "adders fang'd" (as Hamlet later calls them) but because they have by now willingly and happily – and, I am suggesting, quite innocently – placed themselves under an "obligation" to the King and Queen. They know the King would not be pleased if Hamlet discovered they had been "sent for". What they cannot foresee is that as soon as Hamlet finds this out he will think of them as spies, and never trust them again.

We might wonder what is so wrong with their coming when "sent for". When teaching *Hamlet* in Japan I asked a group of postgraduates what they would have done if they had become friends with the Emperor's son and then received a summons from the concerned Imperial couple. They replied that they would have accepted such an invitation because they wanted to help their friend.

Rosencrantz replies to Hamlet's seemingly casual question truthfully, if carefully: "To visit you, my lord, no other occasion." Hamlet sees through this immediately and becomes frighteningly aggressive:

Were you not sent for? Is it your own inclining?
Is it a free visitation? Come, deal justly with me.

Come, come. Nay, speak.

Hamlet has seen at once how the expressions on their faces give them away. When he then craftily claims to "know the good king and queen have sent for you", the unnerved Rosencrantz becomes even more foolish by trying to be clever: "To what end my lord?" Hamlet replies, witheringly, by speaking of "the rights of our fellowship" and "the obligation of our ever-preserved love" – although we might notice that he is only concerned with what his old school-fellows owe to *him*, not with anything that he might owe old friends. The confounded Rosencrantz appeals to Guildenstern: "What shall we say?" Guildenstern's reply is no less distressed, but not at all silly: "What should we say, my lord?" He has seen how Hamlet is evidently but, arguably, unreasonably convinced that if they were "sent for" they cannot be trusted as true friends. And he admits: "My lord, we were sent for."

Hamlet gives his old friends no chance to explain their arrival in Elsinore. He doesn't ask them *why* they think they were sent for. Instead, he deliberately deceives the friends he no longer trusts when he cautiously describes his affliction as though it has come from nowhere: "of late, but wherefore I know not..."

But then something extraordinary happens, with Hamlet suddenly throwing this caution to the winds and recklessly telling Rosencrantz and

Guildenstern that "my uncle-father and aunt-mother are deceived". "In what my dear lord?" Guildenstern asks, and Hamlet replies: "I am but mad north-north-west. When the wind is southerly, I know a hawk from a handsaw." He is saying that he has deliberately "deceived" the King and Queen by making them suppose that he is mad at all "points of the compass", when he isn't – but why? Any further discussion of this crucial question becomes impossible because at this point Polonius arrives to say that the Players are just behind him.

As the Cambridge critic Theodore Redpath observed in the most searching discussion I have found of Hamlet's changing relationship with his old friends:

> Had they told Claudius just what they had learned up till then, we may be pretty sure that he would have packed Hamlet off before he could do any mischief. But they don't.

Nor do Rosencrantz and Guildenstern betray Hamlet when they next meet the King, though their love and regard for their old friend diminishes in a way that the play carefully charts – and their diminishing regard parallels the changes in Claudius's own sense of how dangerous it is to let Hamlet's "madness range".

We see the change progressing in this same scene (2.2), when Hamlet – preparing to bait

Polonius again – shocks his friends by telling them he will show them "a great baby", not yet out of his "swaddling clouts". He shocks them again, far more deeply, with his behaviour in the Mousetrap scene, when they find themselves watching a play in which a nephew (not a brother) murders his royal uncle, and watch in helpless horror as Hamlet's own performance in his running commentary not only ruins that of the actors but finally menaces his own royal uncle – after he has humiliated Ophelia in an appallingly cruel and public way, and then insulted the Queen no less grossly. From now on their loyalties are divided.

Shortly after this, when Hamlet contemptuously calls them "sponges", Guildenstern dares to tell him that his "courtesy is not of the right breed", and when Hamlet asks "Have you any further trade with us?" the more emotional Rosencrantz protests: "My lord, you once did love me." Minutes later, when they next see Claudius and he very bluntly says, with a kind of relief, "I like him not", they are evidently disposed to agree that it is no longer safe to let Hamlet's madness "range" and agree to escort him to England.

Then, when Hamlet butchers Polonius, they become completely loyal to the King. The big question, of course, is whether they are willing accomplices to Claudius's later plan to have Hamlet killed in England. Hamlet assumes that they are when he arranges that his old friends will suffer the same fate that Hamlet wished, after the Mousetrap, to arrange for the King. They are to be killed immediately, with no "shriving" time allowed, meaning they are condemned to a fate as dreadful as the "unaneled" death of Hamlet's father.* But, as Theodore Redpath concludes, there is no evidence whatever to justify Hamlet's assumption of their guilt.

Claudius decides, or appears to decide, that Hamlet must die at the beginning of Act Four. After Hamlet leaves, "tugging" Polonius's corpse with him, Gertrude tells Claudius that the "mad" Hamlet has killed "the unseen good old man" in a "lawless fit" and the appalled Claudius immediately sees the danger this presents: "His liberty is full of threats to all." He confirms his intention to have Hamlet killed in England in a short soliloquy at the end of Act Four, scene three – "Do it England..." – but does not tell Rosencrantz and Guildenstern what he intends.

John Gielguid believed the other characters in *Hamlet* are "second-rate". A far more appropriate description, perhaps, would be "ordinary". Rosencrantz and Guildenstern are ordinary young

---

* *To die without having "shriving" time means to die without having time to confess your sins to a priest. The terms used by the Ghost in 1.5, such as "unaneled", have a very Catholic flavour. To anele means to administer the last anointing or extreme unction to the dying. It is carried out by a priest who at the same time recites a liturgy to ensure the soul's health as the dying man prepares for Judgement. (See* Shakespeare's Ideas: More Things in Heaven and Earth, *by David Bevington)*

men, by no means unintelligent, and decent. They are never guilty of the kind of betrayal Hamlet imagines when he is – to borrow Granville-Barker's wonderfully blunt phrase – "off his head". His mind and judgement are deranged by his loathing of Claudius when he battily supposes that since they were "sent for" they must be "spies" not his "excellent good friends". He is equally deranged when, later, he discovers the letters they are carrying to the boat on which he will travel with them to England. These letters condemn him to death. But the "packet" in which the letters come is "sealed": there is no evidence that Rosencrantz and Guildenstern know the contents. Yet Hamlet determines to send them to their atrocious deaths.

We do not learn the details of what Hamlet has planned for his former friends until the beginning of the final scene. Then, at the end of this scene, when Hamlet is dead and the stage is littered with corpses, English ambassadors arrive to announce that "Rosencrantz and Guildenstern are dead". This in itself would seem likely to guarantee that Horatio's final pious and loving prayer – that "flights of angels" will sing Hamlet to "his rest" – is, to say the least, unlikely to be answered.

Roy Battenhouse's
"Ten Questions on *Hamlet*"

1. The most important question is the one Hamlet poses on meeting the Ghost: "Be thy intents wicked or charitable...?" (1.4). But since Hamlet never pursues and thus never answers this question, the play challenges us to decide it from evidence given by the Ghost's behaviour and speech and the resulting effect on Hamlet.

2. What defects do you see in the quality of Hamlet's love? What kind of ideal influences his attitudes toward his father, his mother, and Ophelia?

3. Is Claudius as bestial as Hamlet supposes? And are Rosencrantz and Guildenstern "adders fang'd" who deserve to be blown to the moon (3.4)?

4. Is Hamlet's "Mousetrap" a success or a failure? Does it cause Claudius to rush squealing from the room, as a critic such as Dover Wilson supposes? Or, on the contrary, does Claudius exit with a peremptory dignity to give notice of royal disapproval of Hamlet's mischievous use of drama?

5. Is Hamlet's madness real or feigned? Is his "antic disposition" (1.5) a mere mask resorted to (as in Saxo Grammaticus's version of the story) for hiding a political purpose until Hamlet can find opportunity to make himself king by destroying a usurper?

6. How satisfactory do you find Hamlet's "repentance" after killing Polonius? Or his apology to Laertes in Act 5?

7. Why does Hamlet delay in carrying out the Ghost's command? Is he hampered by external circumstances?

8. Can Ophelia's tragedy be traced in part to family advice? How does her later madness differ from Hamlet's?

9. When Horatio asks "flights of angels" to sing Hamlet to his rest can we infer that the dying prince will go to heaven a saved soul? Producers of the play have sometimes suggested this by ending the drama with Horatio's "flights of angels" speech.

10. How do the three sons – Hamlet, Laertes, and Fortinbras – resemble or differ from one another as avengers?

Why does the Mousetrap fail?

As Hamlet explains in his soliloquy at the end of Act Two, after asking the Players to perform "The Murder of Gonzago" with an inserted speech that he himself will write, his play will function as a test. If it is a success, it will establish whether the Ghost can be trusted – by establishing whether Claudius is guilty.

> *I'll have these players*
> *Play something like the murder of my father*

HAMLET AND TROILUS AND CRESSIDA

In *Shakespeare: The Invention of the Human* (1998) Harold Bloom describes *Troilus and Cressida,* the play which Shakespeare wrote immediately after *Hamlet,* as "anti-tragedy, anti-comedy, anti-history". Bloom is right, though he is surely understating the case, when he says that "Something of the aura of *Hamlet* lingers in *Troilus and Cressida*". Indeed it does. In *Shakespeare the Thinker* (2007) , A. D. Nuttall goes further, beginning his discussion as follows:

Troilus and Cressida: Hamlet's Play

Hamlet is a sick, clever man. *Troilus and Cressida* is a sick, clever play. So, clearly, Hamlet is the author of *Troilus and Cressida*– or, at least, *Troilus and Cressida* is the play Hamlet could have written. ■

Before mine uncle. I'll observe his looks,
I'll tent him to the quick. If 'a do blench,
I know my course. The spirit that I have seen
May be a devil... I'll have grounds
More relative than this. (2.2)

When Peter Hall first assembled the actors who were to take part in his 1965 RSC *Hamlet*, he told them that in this production the Mousetrap would fail. I think he was right. Hamlet's Mousetrap should always fail, in every staging of the play.

In the long tradition of seeing the play through Hamlet's eyes, however, critics almost always supposed the Mousetrap to be a complete success – because Hamlet says it is. But let us examine what really happens before Claudius "rises" and calls for "Lights", terminating the players' performance.

No sooner have the King and Queen entered and taken their seats for the play than Hamlet, declining his mother's invitation to "sit by me", starts tormenting Ophelia in an astonishingly gross way that is all the more cruel because it takes place in front of the assembled court:

HAMLET Lady, shall I lie in your lap?
OPHELIA No my lord.
HAMLET I mean, my head upon your lap?
OPHELIA Ay my lord.
HAMLET Do you think I mean country matters?
OPHELIA I think nothing my lord.

HAMLET That's a fair thought to lie between
maids' legs.
OPHELIA What is, my lord?
HAMLET Nothing.
OPHELIA You are merry my lord.
HAMLET Who, I?
OPHELIA Ay my lord.
HAMLET O God, your only jig-maker. What should
a man do but be merry? For look you how cheerfully
my mother looks, and my father died within's two hours.
OPHELIA Nay, 'tis twice two months
my lord.
HAMLET So long? Nay then let the devil wear
black... (3.2)

The coarse sexual pun in "country matters" would
have been perfectly familiar to the first audiences
(and Ophelia), although modern spectators may
miss the pun on "Nothing" here and in the title of
Much Ado About Nothing: the word "nothing" was
a common slang word for what lies "between
maid's legs". Like her father earlier, poor Ophelia
has no recourse. She is only her father's daughter,
not his son, although we might wonder whether
Hamlet would be behaving in this vile way if
Laertes were present.

When Hamlet says "look you how cheerfully
my mother looks", he is already lining her up as his
next target, but she is temporarily spared when the
"hoboys play" and "the dumb-show enters". As

Mary Springfels noted in a good *Encyclopaedia Britannica* essay on "Music in Shakespeare's Plays", while the sounds of the lute and *viol* were perceived "to act like benign forces" that "eased melancholy", shawms or "hoboys" (oboes) were ill winds that blew no good; their sounds presaged doom or disaster", as when they "heralded the evil banquets in *Titus Andronicus* and *Macbeth*".

The first important point to note is that Claudius doesn't react at all to the representation of how he murdered Hamlet's father in the dumb show which begins the performance (and puzzles Ophelia).

Hamlet says nothing during the dumb show, but once the spoken play starts he provides an increasingly hectic running commentary that insults the Queen in public. Since critics who see the play and its other characters through Hamlet's eyes so often see Gertrude as a rather vacuous pleasure-loving woman or as Bradley's "sheep in the sun", it is worth noting her dry reply to Hamlet's pointed question "Madam, how like you this play?": "The lady doth protest too much methinks." She is impressively self-possessed, whereas her son is by this time flying out of control.

Still, Gertrude cannot but be hurt and horrified by what is happening, and it gets worse and worse. As Michael Pennington observes, the Player Queen's lines

In second husband let me be accurst

are "like a bucket of dirty water thrown at her",
before her son "interrupts to rub home the point
– "wormwood, wormwood!"

Three lines later the Player Queen says it again:

A second time I kill my husband dead
When second husband kisses me in bed.

Pennington writes:

> Claudius should really stop the play now and
> retreat with dignity, surrounded by his
> scandalized court. But sympathy may be
> accumulating for Gertrude and himself; and there
> could be something to be gained from seeing how
> far up the leg Hamlet can shoot himself.

Hamlet himself has almost brought the play to a
halt by the time Claudius finally speaks and asks
Hamlet: "Have you heard the argument? Is there
no offence in't?" The actor playing the murderer
Lucianus cannot enter until Hamlet has finished
his lengthy reply to Claudius, and then, when the
poor actor does come on, Hamlet explains that
Lucianus is the "nephew to the king" – as Hamlet
is the nephew of Claudius. There is offence enough
in that to horrify the onstage audience, whether or
not Claudius preserves his self-control.

Laurence Olivier and Eileen Herlie in the 1948 multi-award winning 1948 adaptation of Hamlet

After this thunderbolt, which sounds like a thinly veiled threat, the actor still can't begin. He has to wait until Hamlet finishes another viciously misogynistic outburst against Ophelia (once again showing how, as A.D. Nuttall says, he has become "incapable of having normal sexual relations with any woman") and then has the breathtaking effrontery to tell "Lucianus" to get on with the play:

> *Begin, murderer. Pox, leave thy damnable faces and begin. Come, the roaking raven doth bellow for revenge.*

81

The poor actor manages to speak six lines and pour the poison into his uncle's (not his brother's) ears, before Hamlet takes over again to deliver his next and last thunderbolt:

> *A poisons him i'th'garden for's estate.*
> *His name's Gonzago. The story is extant, and written*
> *in very choice Italian. You shall see anon how the*
> *murderer gets the love of Gonzago's wife.*

At this point Claudius finally has to call a halt. Hamlet's astonishing performance hasn't just ruined that of the Players, it has ruined what was to be a test. That Claudius puts a stop to it doesn't establish his guilt; he would surely have to stop this appalling "entertainment" even if he were entirely innocent.

This poses a problem for all those critics who see the play through Hamlet's eyes, since Hamlet is so convinced that his Mousetrap is a success and establishes Claudius's guilt. But how could it do that?

John Dover Wilson's account of "what happens" when the King "rises" reads like an extract from the script for the 1948 film Sir Laurence Olivier had not yet made:

Terrified by the thought that "Hamlet knows all!", [Claudius] pulls himself to his feet, and, squealing for light, he totters as fast as his trembling knees will take him from the terrible, the threatening room. King Mouse has become a shambling, blinking paddock.

In *Shakespearean Tragedy*, A. C. Bradley had similarly maintained that "Hamlet's device proves a triumph far more complete than he had dared to expect":

> He had thought that the King might "blench", but he [Claudius] does much more. When only six of the "dozen or sixteen lines" have been spoken he starts to his feet and rushes from the hall, followed by the whole dismayed Court.

This idea that Claudius is finally unable to control himself resurfaces yet again in the Norton edition of Shakespeare when Stephen Greenblatt writes: "after the King has stormed out in a rage..." But Bradley, Dover Wilson and Greenblatt are all *inventing* stage directions which they then treat as part of Shakespeare's text. The text itself, on the other hand, confirms that the traditional way of reading and staging this scene must be wrong, for two different but related reasons.

First, Shakespeare's Claudius never supposes that Hamlet "knows all", as Dover Wilson claims. When he is struggling to pray in the next scene he clearly does *not* suppose that Hamlet or anybody else, apart from God, knows or could know what he has done. Far from speaking like a man who has just betrayed his guilt in public, he expresses no fear that anything in "this world" might make it difficult or impossible for him to "retain" those "effects for which I did the murder, / My crown, mine own ambition, and my queen" (3.3).

Secondly, if Claudius had betrayed his guilt, it is likely this would have been obvious to other characters, not only to Hamlet. Yet the other characters who express a view all speak as though what they had seen – both in the play-within-a-play and in Hamlet's increasingly insulting running commentary – was a nephew killing or threatening to kill his royal uncle.

Productions that ignore these awkward but demonstrable textual facts become incoherent. So, for example, in Peter Wirth's 1961 film version with the excellent Maximilian Schell, Gertrude

CRITICS AND THE MOUSETRAP

The first writer to suggest that the Mousetrap fails to establish Claudius's guilt was the Japanese novelist Shiga Naoya – in a brilliant short story, "Claudius's Diary" (1912). Naoya didn't share in the general enthusiasm for Hamlet and found Claudius more admirable, rejecting the idea that the Mousetrap established Claudius's guilt. This provided the assumptive basis for his story, which is told from the point of view of the increasingly disturbed Claudius. Unfortunately Shiga was so fired by this that he undermined his argument by going on to publish an essay

looks at Claudius "in shock and dismay" as she "finally begins to suspect what her doting husband may have done to win her". This may have seemed like an inspired moment of "good theatre", which so often betrays great drama with a Judas kiss. But if Shakespeare's Gertrude really suspects that Claudius murdered her first husband she would have to be even more brazenly, chillingly self-possessed than Lady Macbeth when she reproaches Hamlet for having "much offended" his "father" – meaning Claudius.

Similarly, the Mousetrap scene in Zeffirelli's film of *Hamlet* shows Ian Holm's thunderstruck Polonius suddenly guessing what Claudius has done, but can we seriously suppose that Polonius would then speak as he does to Claudius in their last

arguing that Claudius was really innocent.

But on the Mousetrap he was right. As Anne Barton has emphasised, Hamlet "lacks real evidence of his uncle's villainy" until Act Four, when he discovers the letter of commission that Rosencrantz and Guildenstern are carrying. This letter is what also convinces Horatio, when he finally exclaims: "Why, what a king is this!"

Another critic who argued that the Mousetrap fails was the redoubtable W. W. Greg, writing a few years later, in 1917. Unfortunately he, too, is less sound on other matters, believing, for example, that the Ghost is a "hallucination". The objection is obvious: the Ghost is seen 11 times by four different characters. But Greg argued, unconvincingly, that we should regard this fact as "a freak of collective suggestion, and explain it away as we should any other spook". ∎

meeting – when he assures the King that the Queen will take her son to task ("I warrant she'll tax him home") – or have the effrontery to tell the Queen that her son's "pranks have been too broad to bear with"? Pranks? And if Rosencrantz and Guildenstern suspected that the King had killed King Hamlet, they would never dare to babble to Claudius about the "cess of majesty" and their own "Most holy and religious fear". They are terribly shocked by what they have seen. As I have already suggested, this is the point where their loyalty switches to the King, even before Hamlet butchers Polonius.

Why doesn't Hamlet listen to Horatio?

It may seem absurd to suggest that *Hamlet* shows how Prince Hamlet lacks imagination, but in one specific, demonstrable sense that's exactly what it does. Although Hamlet is so passionately eloquent about his own thoughts and feelings, he isn't interested in – and rarely tries to imagine or ascertain – what *anybody else thinks and feels*. The most telling contrast here is with the play itself, which includes other tragedies besides that of the Prince, taking us "inside" all the principal characters and showing us how they think and feel.

After what he believes to be the complete success of the Mousetrap in establishing Claudius's guilt, Hamlet sings a song and crows to Horatio that he now deserves a "fellowship", or full partner's share, in a company of players (3.2) because he himself has arranged their performance so well. Horatio, however, replies "Half a share". He is intimating that he doesn't agree with Hamlet. He might think that the Mousetrap has *not* established Claudius's guilt as conclusively as Hamlet supposes, or he might think that even if Claudius is guilty Hamlet is wrong to trust the Ghost and, in Hamlet's phrase, "take its word for a thousand pound".

As we have seen, both of these doubts would be reasonable, but we never learn what Horatio thinks because Hamlet doesn't ask him – even though he has earlier told Horatio that he wanted the two of them to compare their responses once the Mousetrap has been performed. Instead, when Horatio says "Half a share", the triumphantly insouciant Hamlet replies "A whole one I", and starts singing again.

Similarly, when Hamlet later tells Horatio how he has arranged that when Rosencrantz and Guildenstern arrive in England they will be "put to sudden death", without even being allowed "shriving time" in which to confess and receive absolution, Horatio's response is guarded: "So Rosencrantz and Guildenstern go to't" (5.2). The

hint of shock or disapproval is enough to prompt
Hamlet's self-justifying reply:

Why man, they did make love to this employment.
They are not near my conscience.

Yet this reply once again dismisses whatever
reservations Horatio may have. Horatio might well
think it wicked of Hamlet to try to make God his
instrument in securing the worst possible
punishment for Rosencrantz and Guildenstern.
He might think the sealed letter that Rosencrantz
and Guildenstern were carrying is not sufficient
evidence that they were willing accomplices to
Hamlet's murder. The Hamlet who so famously
claims to have "that within which passes show"
isn't at all concerned with what Horatio has
"within". He doesn't ask Horatio what he thinks.

For the same reason we can never know what
and how Gertrude thinks and feels in the closet
scene after Hamlet kills Polonius. As noted earlier,
Gertrude is stunned by the suggestions that
Claudius may have murdered his father. "A bloody
deed?" he says after the death of Polonius:

Almost as bad, good mother,
As kill a king and marry with his brother. (3.3)

Gertrude can only echo him: "As kill a king?" Since
Hamlet doesn't answer her question or pursue the

point, she may still be unaware at the end of this scene that her second husband killed the first. This is indeed "extraordinary", as the critic Philip Edwards says.

Since his encounter with the Ghost, Hamlet has been desperate to know the extent of his mother's guilt or innocence; before this point he has never suggested she might have been an accomplice to the murder. But instead of replying to Gertrude he lifts the arras, to see whether the man he has just killed is the King. When he then sees Polonius he expresses his contempt for the "wretched, rash, intruding fool". It never occurs to him, at this moment or later, to wonder or imagine what will now happen to the fatherless Ophelia, even though his mother, Ophelia and Horatio are the only characters Hamlet could be said to love, apart from his dead father and, long ago, Yorick.

"Nothing in this play," says Philip Edwards,

is more bizarre than that Hamlet, having committed the terrible error of killing Polonius, should be so consumed with the desire to purge and rescue his mother that he goes right on with the castigation [of her] even with the dead body of Polonius at his feet... Poor Polonius. Hamlet is at his worst in these scenes. His self-righteousness expands in his violent rebukes of his mother and his eagerness to order her sex-life.

Of course Hamlet hasn't always been like this. He has changed, profoundly. He is in no way to blame for the suffering he has been caused. His world has died and with it his capacity to imagine what Horatio or his mother or Ophelia might be thinking or feeling. I think Anne Barton is right that we go on loving and caring for Hamlet throughout the play, despite his behaviour.

But it is not easy to sympathise with his behaviour in the scenes we are discussing. When, on the way to meet his mother, Hamlet comes upon Claudius on his knees and refrains from stabbing him his fear is that if he does so Claudius *may not be damned.*

It is just before this, when Claudius's prayer begins, that we hear and know *for the first time* what the Mousetrap has failed to establish: that Claudius did indeed murder his royal brother, Hamlet's father:

> *Oh, my offence is rank, it smells to heaven;*
> *It hath the primal eldest curse upon't,*
> *A brother's murder.*

The Ghost had commanded Hamlet to kill Claudius and leave his mother to the pricks and stings of conscience, but it is Claudius, here, who feels the agonies of conscience. When Gertrude breaks down in the next scene it is with shame and guilt: her son has found out her dreadful secret –

that she was Claudius's lover before Hamlet's father died. Claudius's agony is different. He is sure that nobody on earth, including Hamlet, knows he has committed the "primal sin" that Cain committed when he murdered his brother Abel. But he is racked by his belief that God knows what he has done.

> *What then? What rests?*
> *Try what repentance can. What can it not?*
> *Yet what can it when one cannot repent?*

In the "corrupted currents of this world", Claudius reflects,

> *oft 'tis seen the wicked prize itself*
> *Buys out the law. But 'tis not so above...*

where there "is no shuffling" (or making excuses). Nor is there is any "shuffling" in this soliloquy, which is the most profoundly Christian speech in the play. It is this speech which makes us sense, for the first time, that Claudius is a potentially tragic figure and a forerunner of Macbeth. Like Macbeth, he is determined to hold on to what he has gained, and, like Macbeth, he thus finds himself propelled towards a second murder.

It is at this momentous moment that Hamlet enters. He does not have to stab the defenceless King in the back while he is praying. He could confront or challenge him. Instead, he delivers his sixth "Now might I do it pat" soliloquy, which is full of "shuffling". Hamlet does not consider how God might judge him. His only concern is to work 'the system' – or what, according to the Ghost, is the divine or infernal 'system' – by killing Claudius at some moment "that has no relish of salvation in't", so that "his heels may kick at heaven" and "his soul may be as damned and black / As hell whereto it goes". This, said the profoundly Christian Dr Johnson, is "too terrible to be read or to be uttered".

"Perhaps the contagion of hell *has* touched Hamlet," says Philip Edwards. But though we may be appalled by the way Hamlet wants Claudius to go to hell, it is perhaps even more striking that he feels he has the power to control the fate of Claudius's soul. One doesn't need to be Christian to agree with Edwards that in this scene "the arrogance of the man who is trying to effect justice is strongly contrasted with the Christian humility of the man who has done murder".

The terrible irony of Hamlet's decision to ignore Horatio's doubts and act like Providence, seeking to control the destinies of both Claudius and Gertrude, is that he ends up killing the wrong man and in doing so initiates another cycle of revenge for a murdered father (Laertes for Polonius), a cycle of revenge which leads directly to the final catastrophe.

Meanwhile, he has driven Ophelia first to madness and then to what is almost certainly suicide. In Act Five, Scene One, when he holds up the skull of the dead jester, Yorick, and reflects on the vanity of life and the inevitability of death, his truths, as Edwards puts it, are based on "a chasm of ignorance". He doesn't know that the grave over which he is speaking has been prepared for Ophelia, for whose death he is responsible. He utters no word of regret for the misery he has caused her, not least by killing her father. And when Laertes leaps into the grave to express his love for her, and Hamlet then claims "I loved Ophelia – with a love forty thousand brothers could not match", it's hard to take the claim seriously. Laertes, unlike Hamlet, approaches revenge in a simple and straightforward way – they are more or less opposites in the way they act and think – and Laertes schemes to kill the Prince with a dreadful trick. But Shakespeare refuses to let us despise him: in the graveyard scene we are more inclined to believe Laertes's protestations of love for Ophelia than we are to believe Hamlet's.

By this stage of the play, indeed throughout the final act, we have no access to his inner thoughts. After his last soliloquy in Act Four, scene four, which finishes

Oh from this time forth,
My thoughts be bloody, or be nothing worth!

we see him only from the outside, losing our privileged access to his innermost thoughts, feelings, and confusions. Hamlet is now convinced heaven is guiding him and that the removal of Claudius is a task he must perform at the risk of his soul, and critics who want to see a religious or spiritual development in the play have seized on his remarks about the "divinity that doth shape our ends" and on his later, longer speech about there being "special Providence in the fall of a sparrow".

The first remark, however, is undercut at once, and very savagely, by what Hamlet then tells Horatio: that he has sent Rosencrantz and Guildenstern to their deaths. If any divinity helped Hamlet to shape the ends of these two innocent men, it must have been infernal. As I have argued, Rosencrantz and Guildenstern are more important in the play than most critics allow, something which is underlined by the way Shakespeare holds back the horrible details of their fate until the final scene. The lines about the sparrow and providence are moving because Hamlet so obviously has a premonition that he may die now. But far from suggesting any kind of benign or helpful divine intervention, they suggest at most that God observes without interfering with the workings of Nature.

And in this case, once again, what immediately follows is another glimpse of Hamlet at his worst, when he apologises to Laertes. The apology is

Kenneth Branagh as Hamlet in the 1996 film adaptation. Branagh also directed the film

appalling, as many commentators have noted: Hamlet refuses to take any responsibility for what he has done, absolving himself by blaming his "madness". Here the contrast with Greek tragedy seems to me very telling. On the whole the Greeks got by very well without inventing the modern conception of "free will". Greek tragic heroes like Oedipus and Ajax are not responsible for their terrible crimes, since they are possessed ("atē", to use the Greek word) by vengeful gods or goddesses. But they become tragic heroes when they nonetheless *do* take responsibility for their actions. That, of course, is the very opposite of

95

what Hamlet is doing in his thoroughly dishonest, ignoble and untragic "apology" to Laertes.

Hamlet, like the Shakespearean tragedies which follow it, suggests that what we think of as the "self" is highly fragile and vulnerable. All of us, as modern cognitive science has confirmed, have not so much one single self as a succession of different selves, and some shocking event, such as befalls Hamlet, can utterly change, even transform us. Othello becomes almost unrecognisable from the idealistic and upright soldier we first encounter; Macbeth turns into a monster. In Hamlet's case the change is equally dramatic. Very poignantly, when the crazed Ophelia recalls the folk tale about the baker's daughter whom Jesus turned into an owl, she says: "Lord we know what we are, but know not what we may be..." (4.5).

When we first encounter Hamlet he is an innocent victim. After the Mousetrap, his attempt to restore "the beauteous majesty of Denmark" ends in disaster, and the extent of his failure is hard to exaggerate. He is in the end responsible, directly or indirectly, not just for the death of Claudius but for the deaths of Polonius, Ophelia, Rosencrantz and Guildenstern, Laertes and his mother, as well, of course, as himself. What's more, far from restoring "the beauteous majesty of Denmark", his one and only act as King elect is to hand his country over to a predatory and hot-headed foreigner – Fortinbras.

Why does Fortinbras matter?

In French the name Fortinbras would mean "strong in arm", suggesting a character with more brawn than brain, just as Hotspur's name or nickname in *Henry IV, Part I* suggests that he has a dangerously short fuse, especially where his obsession with "honour" is concerned.

In *Hamlet* there is no evidence whatever to suggest that the less intelligent and far less sympathetic Fortinbras is in the least concerned with "honour". In the first scene Horatio describes Fortinbras with distaste as a thuggish hothead who is not yet King but is already a threat to his own country as well as Denmark: "Of unimproved mettle hot and full", he has "Sharked up a list of landless resolutes" to serve as his soldiers.

Fortinbras's immediate aim is to recover the Norwegian lands that his father had lost, together with his life, when he challenged King Hamlet of Denmark to single combat. King Hamlet's now legendary, medievally-toned triumph had a cost, in the threat of payback that has now surfaced 30 years later. As the sentry Barnardo says, King Hamlet's triumph "was and is the question of these wars" – that is, the cause of a dispute that has now finally surfaced in the threat of a Norwegian invasion.

The recently crowned King Claudius has no

time for chivalry, honour and all that medieval stuff, and certainly isn't going to march off with a poleaxe. Instead, he shows his mastery of the new Renaissance or Machiavellian art of what would later be called *Realpolitik* when he works out the best way of cutting off the funds that Fortinbras needs to pay his soldiers. No money, no honey. Or, to put that more positively, the new King of Denmark is arguably far more concerned to protect his country and his subjects than the old one was.

When the redoubtable King Hamlet slew his redoubtable challenger, all of the unfortunate Norwegians who then became Danish subjects were doubtless made very unhappy. But if King Hamlet had *lost* after taking up King Fortinbras's challenge, numberless Danes would have become Norwegian subjects and equally unhappy. The risks, however, didn't seem to concern either of them. Horatio obviously disapproves of old King Fortinbras when he says that he was "pricked on by a most emulate pride", but his contrast with "our most valiant Hamlet" looks more like special pleading, or a distinction without a difference, when he adds: "For so this side of our known world esteemed him."

Young Fortinbras has been a significant and often ominous figure in European productions of *Hamlet*, by directors like Andrzej Wajda and Ingmar Bergman. If, like Wajda, you lived in Poland – which for a century and a half existed only as a passionately preserved idea but not, after the three partitions, as a country – your response when Shakespeare's play shows a Norwegian taking over the Danish throne is likely to be more disturbed than that of an American, whose country hasn't been invaded since 1492. The play's first English audiences would have felt a similar sense of anxiety, given the worries that then existed about the succession to the throne – and what would happen after the old and ailing Queen Elizabeth's death.

To eliminate Fortinbras is to block out the play's political dimension. Yet Fortinbras was regularly eliminated from the end of the play in all of the English stagings of *Hamlet* from 1718, or earlier, until Bernard Shaw persuaded the thoughtful actor Sir Johnston Forbes-Robertson to reinstate Shakespeare's political ending. (Shaw would never have tried to persuade the more celebrated Henry Irving to do this: he told Ellen Terry that Irving was "absolutely the stupidest man I ever met".)

Nonetheless, Fortinbras continued to be eliminated in some later English stagings and in filmed versions of the play such as Laurence Olivier's. More recently, the Royal Shakespeare Company's 2008 production ended with Horatio piously hoping that flights of angels sing Hamlet to his rest.

And of course Hamlet himself is entirely, and shockingly, indifferent to the play's political dimension, which is there from the start. Fortinbras doesn't appear until near the end of the play, but we aren't likely to forget Horatio's early speech about the threat of a Norwegian invasion. We remember it because it is long and detailed, and because it is craftily placed in the first scene when Horatio and Marcellus consider whether the Ghost's recent appearances might somehow be connected with Denmark's feverish but mysterious preparations for war. This expository material provides the basis for the play's concern with a question which always preoccupied Shakespeare: what makes a good king?

The only truly *morally* good, indeed saintly king he dramatised is Henry VI, who turned out to be a disaster on the throne. Claudius is a good king in the sense that he is an effective king, as we see in the second scene as he deals cleverly and efficiently with the threat from Norway. Moreover, when Polonius asks him whether he has ever had cause to doubt the political advice he, Polonius, has given in the past, it suggests that Claudius is

HAMLET IN EUROPE

Significantly, the history of *Hamlet* productions on the continent is very different, with sharply critical and even hostile views of the Prince emerging much earlier, in parallel with a tendency to give more emphasis to the Fortinbras plot.

Germany was the first country properly to assimilate Shakespeare, and above all *Hamlet*, to its own culture. Goethe, Germany's greatest poet, famously

experienced at running Denmark – that Hamlet's father, like Prospero in *The Tempest*, would leave his younger brother (not his Queen) in charge when he was away burnishing his legend as a warrior king. Indeed we can assume that this was the chief reason why Claudius, not Prince Hamlet, was elected to be the new King.

Prince Hamlet is not in the least concerned with the fate of Denmark and its people. In his reunion with Rosencrantz and Guildenstern he describes Denmark as a "prison", and when Rosencrantz pertinently comments "Then is the world one", Hamlet replies: "A goodly one, in which there are many confines, wards, and dungeons; Denmark being one o'th'worst."

When he is leaving for England in Act Four, Scene Four, and sees Fortinbras entering Denmark with his army, he doesn't even wonder, or try to imagine, why. And then, in the final act, his first and only action as the designated new Danish king

referred to Shakespeare as "unser Shakespeare", or *our* Shakespeare. Later, August Wilhelm von Schlegel upped that claim by describing Shakespeare as "ganz unser", or *entirely* ours, and by 1839 the German Romantic poet Heinrich Heine was claiming that the Germans "have comprehended Shakespeare better than the English".

But by the 1830s German writers were also taking a far more critical view of the melancholy Dane. When Ferdinand Freiligrath launched his 1844 poem "Deutschland" with the claim that "Deutschland ist Hamlet" (Germany is Hamlet) this identification was not another

is to deliver his country to a foreign power by giving Fortinbras his "dying voice". He might better have saved whatever breath remained, since Fortinbras is not slow to see and seize what he calls his "vantage". Once Fortinbras rules Denmark, it means he will be able to conscript thousands of Danes to fight for some pitiful stretch of land that (as the Norwegian captain says) is not large enough to contain the graves of the dead. Whatever view one takes of the Danish court, the Danish people were safer and much better off under Claudius, just as there are strong suggestions that Gertrude is much happier with her second husband.

John Dover Wilson and even A.C. Bradley seek to justify Hamlet's behaviour by arguing that the Danish court is corrupt. But is it? That the Danish electors have chosen Claudius rather than the Prince as their king is no proof of corruption, while the play's second scene suggests Claudius is conscious of his duty and diligent in performing it.

---

celebratory claim that Germans were best able to understand Hamlet: Freiligrath was claiming that the Germans and German Romanticism were all too like Hamlet in their apolitical introspection and inanition.

A few decades later something strikingly similar happened in Russia. Eleanor Rowe's excellent study *Hamlet: A Window on Russia* shows how, by the 1840s, Hamlet was the darling of the intelligentsia and "Hamletism" was the fashionable pose. Twenty years later, however, Hamlet's strengths and weaknesses were

Finally, we should note how removing Fortinbras from the play has other consequences, since Shakespeare's use of him is typical of his dramatic method. The play sets him alongside Hamlet and Laertes as the three sons (four, if we want to include "Pyrrhus"*) who all react differently to the loss of a father. Fortinbras and Laertes also represent vacuous versions of "honour". In short, although we don't even see Fortinbras until the play is almost over (if we are allowed to see him at all) he figures in an intricately varied crisscrossing of contrasts and significances. To cut him out because politics seems unimportant – meaning that politics and the fate of Denmark aren't important to Hamlet himself – is to miss out an important element of the play.

---

* *In Greek legend Pyrrhus was the son of Achilles, who was killed by Paris in the Trojan war. Pyrrhus, like Hamlet, swears to avenge his father, and, because Paris is already dead, kills his father, Priam, showing no mercy when he does so. (Both Hamlet and the First Player refer to this legend in Act Two, scene two.)*

---

being much more vigorously debated, and Turgenev was publishing his great essay on "Hamlet and Don Quixote" in the same year as his pre-revolutionary novel *On the Eve*.

Some of Turgenev's criticisms of Hamlet's "sickly inanition", "egotism" and "doctrine of negation" were to be echoed (though with less emphasis on politics) by G. Wilson Knight in England in 1930 when he described Hamlet in *The Wheel of Fire* as "the ambassador of death amid life". ∎

How pessimistic is *Hamlet*?

George Wilson Knight's essay "The Embassy of Death" in *The Wheel of Fire* (1930) is justly famous. Although the author subsequently modified his position, the essay departs vigorously from the Hamlet-centric critical tradition and is a striking and original piece of work. Knight argues that Denmark, as shown to us in the play, is in fact a healthy and contented place, with Claudius a kindly and efficient king, and Hamlet a figure of nihilism and death. Yes, Claudius is a murderer and Hamlet has right on his side but which of the two, Knight asks, "is the embodiment of spiritual good, which of evil? The question of the relative morality of Hamlet and Claudius reflects the ultimate problem of this play."

> A balanced judgement is forced to pronounce ultimately in favour of life as contrasted with death, for optimism and the healthily second-rate, rather than the nihilism of the superman: for he is not, as the plot shows, safe; and he is not safe, primarily because he is right.

If Hamlet had acted quickly, then vengeance might have been justifiable, but he doesn't, causing only disaster, so it would have been better if he had forgotten the Ghost's commands – the Ghost, anyway, being nothing but a minor spirit. Quoting Hamlet – "The spirit that I have seen / May be the devil..." – Wilson Knight added: "It was... Or at least... it certainly was no 'spirit of health'."

Knight's argument was hugely influential and a useful antidote to the traditional, Bradleyan view of the play, but it is equally flawed, or, as Philip Edwards puts it, "brilliant and wrong".

The values of the Danish court, as shown in the play, are far from admirable. Claudius, Polonius and Laertes, are "much given to expressing their views in resonant platitudes", as Edwards says. Claudius knows the proper response to death, Laertes to sex, Polonius to everything, but with each one of them "we see the insufficiency of their moralising". Claudius hides the fact that he is a murderer, even from his new wife, who in turn tried to hide her double life from her late husband.

Laertes is suspected by both his sister and his father of an inclination towards the primrose path of dalliance. Polonius advocates reticence, truth and straight dealing, but is loquacious and devious. It is the ever-ready platitudes, betrayed both by their rhetoric and by the conduct of those who utter them, that Hamlet discards as mere "saws of books" as he enters his new life. It is interesting that the heavy moralising of the court party accompanies a low view of human nature.

Polonius and Laertes both expect Hamlet to be the insouciant seducer that is their stereotype of an aristocrat... Polonius's proclivity for spying – which leads to his violent death – is shown in the grotesque commission to Reynaldo to keep an eye on Laertes in Paris and then in his schemes to find out what's wrong with Hamlet.

In her comprehensive study of *Shakespeare's Imagery*, Caroline Spurgeon says that images of disease, tumours, ulcers, abesses, cancer and the like are spread through *Hamlet*, more so than through any other Shakespeare play, reinforcing the impression we get, as she puts it, of the "unwholesome condition" of Denmark. To give but a few examples, Gertrude speaks of her "sick soul" (4.5); Hamlet, earlier, speaks of his mother's sin as a blister on the "fair forehead of an innocent love" (3.4); to have married Claudius, her sense must be not only "sickly" but "apoplex'd"; Hamlet begs her not to believe that the Ghost was due to his madness, and not to see her own guilt, for that

> *will but skin and film the ulcerous place,*
> *Whiles rank corruption, mining all within,*
> *Infects unseen.*

Sturgeon is right that the idea of an ulcer infecting and fatally undermining the body is spread through the play, but most of this imagery, as the

German critic Wolfgang Clemen says in his sensible analysis of the play, comes in Hamlet's speeches and soliloquies. The thought of a body being poisoned, implanted in Hamlet by the Ghost, buries itself deep in his imagination (and indeed poisoning is a major leitmotif of the play from the first act to the last, when all the major characters end up being poisoned). The images Hamlet uses are those of a man "gifted with greater powers of observation [than others]. He is capable of scanning reality with a keener eye and of penetrating the veil of semblance even to the core of things"; he ruthlessly sees through and breaks down the barriers of hypocrisy. But the ulcer images, like those of the unweeded garden, are largely Hamlet's.

And though Claudius is a murderer and an adulterer, the play does not suggest that Denmark is an especially or unusually corrupt country: any functioning society, held up to a gaze as penetrating and intelligent as Hamlet's, is full of hypocricy and dependent on double standards; without them it would quickly fail. Hamlet, says the distinguished American critic Harold Bloom, makes us see the world in ways we may not want to see it. "Elsinore's disease is anywhere's, anytime's. Something is rotten in every state, and if your sensibility is like Hamlet's, then finally you will not tolerate it."

In Shakespeare's play, Hamlet's extraordinary negativity, and his closely related sex nausea, are opposed to the ordinary – to the sense that ordinary people have that ordinary life, to which they remain attached, is better than the alternative, that it is better not to think too deeply, as Hamlet does.

At the heart of the play, as we have seen, is a profound dispute about how we value things – about whether value lies in the person or object being valued, or whether it lies simply in the eyes of the valuer: Hamlet himself expresses the idea that nothing, by itself, has any intrinsic worth when he says, "There is nothing good or bad, but thinking makes it so." It is a thought echoed in the play which Shakespeare wrote immediately after Hamlet, *Troilus and Cressida*. Indeed when Troilus asks, "What's aught, but as 'tis valued?" he sounds like Hamlet's younger, more callow student. The great Trojan debate on values in *Troilus and Cressida* is precipitated by the urgently pressing question of whether the Trojans should go on fighting to keep Helen of Troy, who is, as Hector insists, "not worth / What she doth cost the holding". This develops into a dispute about whether or not values are objective: Hector insists that they are, Troilus asserts that they are not. This dispute, though not so directly, is very much present in *Hamlet*.

"There are no moral facts whatsoever," says Nietzsche in *The Twilight of the Idols*. J. L. Mackie's admirable book on *Ethics* begins: "There are no objective values." The Hamlet who says that

Jude Law as Hamlet in Michael Grandage's 2009 production at the Wyndham's Theatre in London

"Nothing is either good or bad, but thinking makes it so" would agree with that, although most Christians would disagree with Mackie and Hamlet. And Hamlet himself, while he can't suppress the thought that there are no real values, never quite surrenders to the thought: he will never quite deny the baffled aspirations of his own idealistic nature.

In Act Four, scene four, Hamlet hears from Fortinbras's Captain about a Norwegian expedition to take a "little patch of ground" in Poland which is not even worth "five ducats". In the soliloquy that follows, Hamlet throws out two sharply opposed concepts of "honour" without showing how the gulf between them can be bridged. For Hamlet to feel "shamed", as he says he does, by the "example" of Fortinbras's resolution presupposes that the Norwegian expedition should be regarded as something other than an insane waste of life in a worthless cause.

Yet Hamlet *does* draw a shaming contrast between Fortinbras's resolution and what he sees as his own contemptible procrastination; at the same time he suggests that to go to war over a "straw" or an "Egge-shell" is merely a "fantasie and tricke of fame". There is a logical impasse here, for if "honour" is no more than a "fantasie" then the waste of life is absurd.

Despite this, Hamlet is still, by the end of the play, disposed to give Fortinbras his "dying voice" – so the disaster for Denmark which Claudius has wisely and carefully avoided will take place after all, and moreover it will now be possible for Danes as well as Norwegians to be led off to die by the thousand for an "Egge-shell".

Hamlet's tormented soliloquy, however, is also remarkably coherent: what comes through the contradictions, and underlies the twists in the argument, is the intensity of his disgust with himself and the world. It is this disgust which lies behind his attempt to make himself admire Fortinbras's sense of honour, while he himself has come to feel it is meaningless.

In later plays, Shakespeare frequently separates incompatible views on concepts such as honour by presenting them as symbolic confrontations between different characters – Othello and Iago, for example – but in *Hamlet* the conflict is internalised, with the central character torn between opposing views. I am not the first to observe that Hamlet is his own Iago. So strong is the conflict within him that he feels his very hold on life to be shaken by a sickening apprehension of all that is "rank and grosse in Nature". Action, thought Nietzsche, becomes impossible if we know too much:

> Knowledge kills action; action requires the veils of illusion; that is the doctrine of Hamlet... true knowledge, an insight into the horrible truth, outweighs any motive for action...

The play itself offers no answer to Hamlet's dilemma, leaving us with a bleak view of the human condition. Harold Bloom is right: Hamlet, more than any philosopher, makes us see the world in a way we do not want to see it. Bloom is right, too, while acknowledging (as this guide has sought to show) the considerable case *against* Hamlet, that he remains "the Western hero of consciousness": critics who try to dismiss him blow sand against the wind, "and the wind blows it back again..." It does so "despite his crimes and blunders, despite even his brutally pragmatic murderous treatment of Ophelia. *We forgive Hamlet precisely as we forgive ourselves.*" It is hardly surprising that so many critics have seen the play through his eyes: in Shakespeare's time Falstaff may have been more popular, but "the centuries since have preferred the prince not only to the fat knight but to every other fictive being". He dies loving nobody except perhaps Horatio (and, knowing Horatio loves him, is passionately concerned that Horatio should stay alive to heal his wounded name), but "the less he cares for anyone... the more we care for him".

It is Hamlet's view of the human condition which we are left with, expressed so memorably in the most famous of all soliloquies which Bloom calls his "death-speech-in-advance". What we make of the play, however, also depends on what we make of the Ghost, and although this has been ignored or glossed over by countless critics and directors, Shakespeare's text clearly indicates that the Ghost's provenance is uncertain: if it is infernal, then the devil has won; if it is what it says it is – the ghost of Hamlet's father – then that is no more comforting since divine justice, as I suggested earlier, would appear to have the morals of a fruit machine. The characters who die, directly or indirectly, as a result of the Ghost's "dread command" will all suffer the same fate as Rosencrantz and Guildenstern: they will die "unshriven", or unconfessed, condemned to the same unspeakable torments which the Ghost says he himself has suffered. Either way, "flights of angels" will not be singing Hamlet to his rest.

When it was written *Hamlet* was the first great tragedy to appear for nearly 2,000 years, since the great Greek tragedies of Sophocles, Aeschylus and Euripides. We live in an age committed to the meliorist idea that the world can be improved: Marxism, Socialism, Conservatism – all, in their different ways, are meliorist philosophies. Christianity is a meliorist religion. At the heart of *Hamlet* is a different view, the view that nothing – no philosophy, no religion – can improve man's lot and that hope, like honour, is a "fantasie". Wilson Knight's claim that the play is "ultimately in favour of life as contrasted with death" may be true of its characters – all except Hamlet – but the play itself seems to take the opposite, Greek view, the view that "the best thing for a man is not to be born, and if already born, to die as soon as possible", as the mythical Greek figure, Silenius, put it in words which are echoed by Hamlet when he says to Ophelia: "it would've been better if my mother had never given birth to me".

THE MADNESS OF
OPHELIA

"Ophelia – poor Ophelia!" wrote Mrs Jameson in 1879. "Oh far too soft, too good, too fair, to be cast among the briars of this working-day world, and fall and bleed upon the thorns of life! What should be said of her?"

The answer, in the view of most critics, is not much. They have consistently neglected Ophelia, though she has always been a popular figure in literature, popular culture and painting. So what does she represent? Does her madness, as Elaine Showalter asks in "Representing Ophelia: Women, Madness, and the Responsibilities of Feminist Criticism", "stand for the oppression of women in society as well as in tragedy"?

Shakespeare gives us little information on her past; she appears in only five scenes and, unlike Hamlet, does not struggle with moral choices or alternatives. "We can imagine Hamlet's story without Ophelia, but Ophelia literally has no story without Hamlet," as another feminist critic, Lee Edwards, puts it.

Not surprisingly, she has been seen in all sorts of different ways. David Leverenz, in

"The Woman in *Hamlet*", believes her story to be no more than a female subtext to the central tragedy. Hamlet's disgust "at the feminine passivity in himself is translated into violent revulsion against women, and into his brutal behaviour towards Ophelia". Ophelia's suicide, in this theory, becomes "a microcosm of the male world's banishment of the female".

Elaine Showalter is surely right when she argues that Ophelia is much more than just "a metaphor of male experience" – though she is undoubtedly "freighted" with symbolic significance. "Whereas for Hamlet madness is metaphysical... for Ophelia it is a product of the female body and female nature..." On the Elizabethan stage, she would dress in white, decking herself with "fantastical garlands" of wild flowers and enter (according to the stage directions of the Second, so-called Bad, Quarto) "distracted" with "hair down singing". She sings wistful and bawdy ballads, and the flowers, says Showalter, suggest both innocent blossoming and "whorish contamination":

The 'weedy trophies' and phallic 'long purples' which she wears to her death intimate an improper and discordant sexuality that Gertrude's lovely elegy cannot quite obscure.

Dishevelled hair, in Elizabethan drama, was

associated with either madness or rape. Drowning, too, "was associated with the feminine, with female fluidity as opposed to masculine aridity".

If, in Elizabethan times, Ophelia's extreme melancholy was seen as "biological and emotional" in its origins – the result of "erotomania" – she was played more decorously in the 18th century, in line with Dr Johnson's description of her as young, beautiful, harmless and pious. On the Victorian stage, however, the famous actress Ellen Terry turned her into a "psychological study in sexual intimidation, a girl terrified of her father, of her lover, and of life itself" – Terry, says Showalter, was the first to challenge the convention of her being dressed in emblematic white; the first in a line of strong, intelligent Ophelias destroyed by the heartlessness of men.

Freud's theories led to more sensual interpretations – Rebecca West famously or infamously argued that she was not "a correct and timid virgin of exquisite sensibilities" but "a disreputable young woman". Freudian directors hinted at incestuous links between Ophelia and Polonius or between Ophelia and Laertes, and Freudian critics talked of her "dangerous sexuality". In *Hamlet's Absent*

Father (1977), Avi Erlich writes that she is "much more ambiguous than the lovely rose of stage tradition" and argues that *Hamlet* is a play about "a father and son who were weak largely because they were undone, in the son's fantasy, by sexually treacherous women". Since the 1970s, Ophelia has been more sympathetically interpreted. To many feminists, as Showalter puts it, she became "the madwoman as heroine, a powerful figure who rebels against the family" and refuses to speak the language of the "patriarchal order". The fact is there is no "true" Ophelia: she has been seen in different ways at different times, and will continue to be.

'Ophelia' by Sir John Everett Millais, painted in 1851

Changing views on *Hamlet*

1765
Dr Johnson writes of the "useless and wanton cruelty" of Hamlet's treatment of Ophelia and says the scene where Hamlet refrains from killing Claudius at prayer for fear he will go to heaven is "too horrible to be read or to be uttered". Dr Johnson is emphatic about Hamlet's failure. "The apparition left the regions of the dead to little purpose."

1795
Goethe sees Hamlet as inadequate, too sensitive for the task he is told to perform. "A beautiful, pure, noble, and most moral nature, without the strength of nerve which makes the hero, sinks beneath a burden which it can neither bear nor throw off..."

Early 1800s
Coleridge sees Hamlet a man incapable of acting (because he thinks too much), while **Hazlitt** says his speeches and sayings are "as real as our own thoughts... It is *we* who are Hamlet."

1872
Nietzsche argues in *The Birth of Tragedy* that Hamlet's problem is not that he thinks too much but that he thinks too deeply. It is not reflection but *understanding* which prevents action: "the apprehension of truth and it terror".

1904

To **A. C. Bradley**, in his monumental *Shakespearean Tragedy*, Hamlet is a noble, generous youth who procrastinates because of the melancholy caused by his father's death and mother's remarriage. Mainly dismissive of the religious element in the tragedies, he sees Hamlet as a partial exception: "there is... a more decided, though always imaginative, intimation of a supreme power concerned in human evil and good..."

1930

G. Wilson Knight says in *The Wheel of Fire* that Hamlet has been poisoned by grief. He is "a sick soul... commanded to heal" and has become "an element of evil in the state of Denmark".

1952

In "The World of *Hamlet*", **Maynard Mack** argues that the act required of Hamlet, "though retributive justice, is one that necessarily involves the doer in the general guilt". Other critics of the period expressed similar views, questioning the morality of revenge, among them **Nigel Alexander** in *Poison, Play and Duel* (1967), saying that the central question is "how does one deal with such a man [Claudius] without becoming like him". In the same year **Eleanor Prosser**'s *Hamlet and Revenge* takes an extreme view, arguing that ghosts tends to be hallucinations or demons out to ensnare one's soul – and that the play suggests revenge must always be an evil act.

TEN KEY QUOTES

> *Frailty, thy name is woman!*
>
> Hamlet [1.2]

> *Neither a borrower nor a lender be...*
>
> Polonius [1.3]

> *This above all: to thine own self be true.*
>
> Polonius [1.3]

> *There are more things in heaven and earth, Horatio, Than are dreamt of in your philosophy.*
>
> Hamlet [1.5]

> *...there is nothing either good or bad, but thinking makes it so.*
>
> Hamlet [2.2]

> *...brevity is the soul of wit.*
>
> Polonius [2.2]

> *To be or not to be: that is the question.*
>
> Hamlet [3.1]

> *The lady doth protest too much, methinks.*
>
> Gertrude [3.2]

> *When sorrows come, they come not single spies, But in battalions.*
>
> Claudius [4.5]

A SHORT CHRONOLOGY

1514 Saxo Grammaticus's *Gesta Danorum* or *History of Denmark*, telling the story of "The Life of Amleth", the legend on which *Hamlet* is based

1564 Shakespeare born in Stratford-upon-Avon

1576 Amleth legend retold in French in Francois de Belleforest's Tragic Histories

1589 The first Elizabethan version of *Hamlet*, possibly written by Thomas Kyd

1596 Shakespeare's 11-year-old son, Hamnet, dies

1599-1602 Shakespeare's *Hamlet*

1603 First Quarto of *Hamlet* published

1603-4 *Othello*

1604 Second Quarto of *Hamlet*

1605-6 *King Lear, Macbeth*

1616 Shakespeare dies on 23rd April

1623 First Folio of *Hamlet*

FURTHER READING

Barton, Anne, *Shakespeare and the Idea of the Play*, Greenwood, 1962

Bloom, Harold, *Shakespeare: The Invention of the Human*, Penguin, 1998

Bradley, A.C., *Shakespearean Tragedy*, Palgrave Macmillan, 1904

Bradshaw, Graham, *Shakespeare's Scepticism*, Harvester Press, 1987

Edwards, Philip (ed.), *Hamlet*, The New Cambridge Shakespeare, Cambridge University Press, 1985

Everett, Barbara, *Young Hamlet: essays on Shakespeare's tragedies*, Clarendon, 1989

Fender, Stephen, *Renaissance Self-Fashioning: From More to Shakespeare*, Chicago, 1980

Girard, Renee, *Violence and the Sacred*, A&C Black, 2005

Jones, Ernest, *Hamlet and Oedipus*, W.W. Norton & Company, 1954

Knight, G. Wilson, *The Wheel of Fire*, Routledge, 1930

Knights, L.C., *An Approach to Hamlet*, Chatto & Windus, 1960

Kott, Jan, *Shakespeare Our Contemporary*, Doubleday, 1964

Madariaga, Salvador de, *On Hamlet*, Cass, 1964

Nuttall, A.D., *Shakespeare The Thinker*, Yale University Press, 2007

Pennington, Michael, *Hamlet: A User's Guide*, Limelight Editions, 1996

Prosser, Eleanor, *Hamlet and Revenge*, Stanford, University Press, 1967

Spurgeon, Caroline, *Shakespeare's Imagery*, Martino Publishing, 2014

Staites, Bert O., *Hamlet and the Concept of Character*, John Hopkins University Press, 1992

Tanner, Tony, Introduction to *William Shakespeare: Tragedies*, Everyman's Library, 2006

Waldock, A.J.A., *Hamlet: A Study in Critical Method*, Cambridge University Press, 1931

Wilson, John Dover, *Hamlet* (New Cambridge Edition), Cambridge University Press, 1934

INDEX

First published in 2016 by
Connell Guides
Artist House
35 Little Russell Street
London WC1A 2HH

10 9 8 7 6 5 4 3 2 1

Picture credits:
p.21 © Donald Cooper/REX/Shutterstock
p.49 © SNAP/REX/Shutterstock
p.61 © Hess/ANL/REX/Shutterstock
p.67 © Alistair Muir/REX/Shutterstock
p.81 © International/REX/Shutterstock
p.95 © Moviestore/ REX/Shutterstock
p.109 © Alistair Muir/REX/Shutterstock

A CIP catalogue record for this book is available from the British Library.
ISBN 978-1-907776-60-1

Design © Nathan Burton
Assistant Editor and typeset by:
Paul Woodward

Printed in Turkey

www.connellguides.com